TAYLOR SWIFT
SONGBOOK

WELCOME

Taylor Swift is without a doubt one of the most talented and prolific songwriters of her generation, and arguably, of all time. The release of *The Tortured Poets Department* has increased her tally of released songs to over 250, with at least 100 more unreleased tracks that we know of. For any artist, this would be an impressive body of work. In an 18-year career – and particularly when she started out so young – it's an incredible feat.

It is not just the quantity of songs, but the quality; her writing has received record-breaking critical acclaim and commercial success. From her wise-beyond-her-years debut to the intelligent and poetic work she is creating today, Taylor continues to impress and enchant us with her uniquely 'Swiftian' turns of phrase and unbelievably catchy melodies.

In a notoriously fickle industry, relentlessly focused on finding the next big thing, Taylor hasn't just survived – she has thrived. For nearly 20 years, she has been writing songs that really resonate with people, and that has been a key element of her success. Regardless of genre, from country to pop and indie to electronica, the songwriting has remained Taylor's superpower.

Now, in *The Taylor Swift Songbook*, you can explore her entire discography to date: delve into all 11 studio albums, the bonus tracks and everything released 'From the Vault' so far, plus her standalone singles, soundtrack contributions and collaborations with other artists. Explore the recurring themes, motifs and hidden messages within Taylor's music, and find a new appreciation for her masterful songwriting craft. Enjoy!

Disclaimer: This edition went to press on 8 May 2024, before Taylor began the European leg of The Eras Tour. Given the recent release of *The Tortured Poets Department*, there may be subsequent single releases and changes to the tour's core setlist that are not reflected in the tracklist symbol notation.

CONTENTS

SYMBOL KEY

 RELEASED AS A SINGLE*

 DELUXE ALBUM TRACK

 FROM THE VAULT

 ERAS TOUR CORE SETLIST

Main image: Getty Images. Album covers: Big Machine Records and Republic Records. *Includes album, promotional and charity singles.

INSIDE TAYLOR'S SONGWRITING

Exploring the inspirations, the ideas and the craft that make
Taylor's catalogue of over 250 hits so compelling

WORDS BY DAVE SMITH

Taylor Swift has spent nearly 20 years writing songs at a prolific pace, both solo and with trusted collaborators: from any perspective you choose, it's clear that she's been on a career-long mission to express herself through music. Even as a 19-year-old, she told *The Australian*: "It would have really taken a lot of the wind out of my sails, personally, if I'd had to sing words that other people wrote; that would have killed me." Let's take a dive into her long and productive journey as a composer.

Taylor's mother Andrea is, we learn, responsible for her daughter's start as a songwriter. "When I was little, she would indulge my imagination and tell me stories," Taylor told The Boot, adding, "I attribute my fascination with writing and storytelling to that." The family would go to the cinema to watch Disney films and emerge singing the songs, just like any family would. But in the Swifts' case, the young songwriter-to-be would use those tunes as improv material: "I'd be singing every single song from the movie on the car ride home, word for word, and my parents noticed that, once I had run out of words, I would just make up my own."

Poetry followed and, believe it or not, a novel that ran to 350 pages – which will surely become an instant bestseller if it's ever published. Songs of Taylor's own came when she used the parts she played in children's theatre as inspiration; at 12 she was given her first guitar and

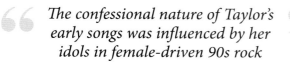

> *The confessional nature of Taylor's early songs was influenced by her idols in female-driven 90s rock*

wrote three songs in two days. An early composition, 'The Outside', was based on her lack of popularity at school, she recalled: "I was a lot different than all the other kids, and I never really knew why. I was taller, and sang country music at karaoke bars and festivals on weekends while other girls went to sleepovers. Some days I woke up not knowing if anyone was going to talk to me that day."

The confessional nature of Taylor's early songs – which carried on into her professional career, of course – was influenced firstly by her idols in female-driven 90s rock, she recalled. "I grew up when Melissa Etheridge and Sarah McLachlan and Alanis Morissette were killing it. Just telling it like it is. And then the Dixie Chicks came along," Taylor told CMT Offstage. "And that made me go, 'Wait. You can sing about your life?'" Her choice of country music as her first genre was a factor, too, that style of music being renowned for encapsulating personal stories in song form.

She retained this openness when it came to songwriting for many years, as well as an accurate understanding that songs aren't made, they seem to appear of their own volition. "It's like this little glittery cloud that floats in front of your face, and you grab it at the right time,' Taylor told the *New York Times* in 2019, adding in an interview with *Harper's Bazaar*: "[It's] the purest part of my job. It can get complicated on every other level, but the songwriting is still the same uncomplicated process it was when I was 12 years old."

TOP Taylor's lyrics often use rain to symbolise sorrow, rebirth, romance and more.
MIDDLE Critics praised the maturity of her early songwriting.
BOTTOM Taylor got her first guitar at the age of 12.

Taylor has a lot of fun incorporating secret messages for fans in her work.

Sometimes, Taylor has revealed, a word or phrase might be enough to kickstart a songwriting session: as she explained, she makes "lists and lists and lists" of words she loves, musing in a speech to students at New York University: "Sometimes a string of words just ensnares me and I can't focus on anything until it's been recorded or written down."

At other times a story, literary or real, might inspire a song – such as Daphne Du Maurier's *Rebecca* and 'tolerate it', or a mother's essay about her son's illness that led to 'Ronan'. We also know that her romantic partners often become immortalised in song – for better or worse, depending on how the relationship fared.

Whatever the subject, Taylor's songwriting style has attracted a lot of praise from various collaborators, with her early co-writer Liz Rose recalling in *Rolling Stone* that her lyrics came at great speed: "She had a story and she wanted to say something specific. She had a lot of information. I just let her go." Ryan Tedder, who worked on 'Welcome to New York' and 'End Game', was similarly impressed, saying: "Taylor is texting you the day before: 'Here are the lyrics, here's a line, here's a melody […] Let's get in, let's do this.' You walk in, and she starts the moment you get in, and you're halfway done with the song by lunch; you're done with it by the end of the day […] Most artists are not that way." Taylor's *folklore* and *evermore* collaborator, Aaron Dessner

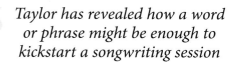

> *Taylor has revealed how a word or phrase might be enough to kickstart a songwriting session*

of The National, spoke of a similar experience of her incredible songwriting pace in a 2023 interview with *Rolling Stone*: "When I sent Taylor the music for our song 'willow' – I think she wrote the entire song from start to finish in less than ten minutes and sent it back to me." A visual record of Taylor's creative flow can be seen on YouTube, in which she composes the lyrics for 'Delicate' in real time while producer Max Martin loops the backing track.

Talking of lyrics, Taylor has a fascinating, three-pronged approach to writing, first revealed at the Nashville Songwriter Awards in 2022. "I've never talked about this publicly before because, well, it's dorky," she explained, "But I have secretly established genre categories for the lyrics I write. They are affectionately titled Quill lyrics, Fountain Pen lyrics and Glitter Gel Pen lyrics. This sounds confusing, but I came up with these categories based on what writing tool I imagined having in my hand when I scribbled it down."

She added that Quill lyrics feature old-fashioned vocabulary ("If I was inspired to write it after reading Charlotte Brontë or after watching a movie where everyone is wearing poet shirts and corsets"), Fountain Pen lyrics are modern but poetic ("Trying to paint a vivid picture of a situation… The love, the loss, everything. The songs I categorise in this style sound like confessions scribbled and sealed in an envelope, but too brutally honest to send"), and Glitter Gel Pen lyrics are "frivolous, carefree, bouncy… [like] the drunk girl at the party who tells you that you look like an angel in the bathroom".

TOP The 'colour' of love is a common motif in Taylor's songs.
MIDDLE Taylor has a talent for making the personal feel universal.
BOTTOM Since moving to New York in 2014, Taylor has referenced the city in several songs.

TOP Taylor's writing has received a great deal of critical acclaim.
MIDDLE Across different genres, her songwriting remains the key.
BOTTOM As a young girl, Taylor always dreamed of sharing her songs with the world.

Taylor's writing style has evolved, of course, as it was bound to do over such a long period of time – which, for context, has been almost twice as long as The Beatles were together. For years, critics described her songwriting essentially as a series of compelling diary entries. There was some truth to that, but only up to a point, as she told the DJ Zane Lowe: "There was a point that I got to as a writer who only wrote very diaristic songs that I felt it was unsustainable for my future moving forward. It felt too hot of a microscope. On my bad days, I would feel like I was loading a cannon of clickbait, when that's not what I want for my life."

Some of her songwriting evolutions were, at heart, reactions to the industry that Taylor is a part of. Take her 2011 song 'Mean', of which she explained to *CMT Offstage*: "This is a song that I wrote about a critic who hated me… In your lowest moment of feeling totally, completely rejected – and like this guy hates you and you can do nothing and you're helpless and you're in this horrible place – and you write a song." She added with a smile, "Then, a year later, you… win two Grammys for it."

The best songwriters use everything as inspiration, including pain – and Taylor is definitely one of those. She spoke to *Rolling Stone* about a particularly tough part of her career: "I thought about how words are my only way of making sense of the world and expressing myself…"

> " *You'll often hear quintessentially Swiftian lyrics mentioning love and heartbreak, fate and karma…* "

she explained. "I wrote a lot of really aggressively bitter poems constantly. I wrote a lot of think pieces that I knew I'd never publish, about what it's like to feel like you're in a shame spiral… Should I just smile all the time and never say anything hurts me? Because that's really fake. Or should I be real about how I'm feeling and have valid, legitimate responses to things that happened to me in my life?"

So where does this leave us? With a large catalogue of released songs by any standards – more than 250 over the course of 18 years, as of May 2024 – meaning that a huge area of ground, musical and lyrical, has been covered. Are there any repeated motifs that make them recognisably 'Taylor' songs? Yes indeed: you'll often hear quintessentially Swiftian lyrics involving love and heartbreak, colours, her favourite cities, the rain, fate and karma to name a few. Taylor also sets many of her songs at the dead of night, with the BBC noting upon the release of 2022's *Midnights* that several of her earlier songs – 'Breathe', 'Enchanted' and 'I Wish You Would' – occur at 2am. Perhaps this is because, like so many of us, the vivid self-analysis that inspires so many of Taylor's songs comes to her when she can't sleep in the early hours, just as it does for the rest of us.

As Taylor told *Songwriter Universe*, "The more it seems like a journal entry, the better. The more it seems like an open letter, the better. The more true and honest and real it gets, the better." If there's a better tip for any budding songwriter than that, we've yet to hear it.

Taylor has established herself as one of the greatest songwriters of her generation.

Taylor's Version
COMING
SOON...

TAYLOR SWIFT

PEAKED AT
NO. 5*

Balancing a maturity beyond her years with youthful naïveté,
Taylor's debut album pointed to a promising future

WORDS BY DAVE SMITH

TIM MCGRAW

WRITERS Taylor Swift, Liz Rose

—

As debut singles go, 'Tim McGraw' is a heck of an achievement, blending understated musicianship with heartfelt lyrics and reaping commercial rewards. Released to US country radio on 19 June 2006, this mostly acoustic ballad invokes the name of McGraw, a renowned country singer, as a way of remembering a nostalgic love affair of the past. The song performed well in various US charts on release, but its real success came years later when it went double platinum – it helped that McGraw himself, later a friend to Taylor, gave it the thumbs up.

PICTURE TO BURN

WRITERS Taylor Swift, Liz Rose

—

Teenage resentment never sounded more fun than on this track, on which Taylor lets fly at a "redneck heartbreaker who's really bad at lying". An upbeat rock song with the expected violins, banjos and other country elements, this chunk of exuberance is pretty much the polar opposite to 'Tim McGraw'. Keep an ear out for the flamboyant chorus, the sound of a person who is not prepared to take any more nonsense from a useless former beau. Reflecting on the song a few years later, Taylor told MTV that she wouldn't express this sentiment in the same way any more: "Now, the way that I would say that and the way that I would feel that kind of pain is a lot different."

Spotlight on...

TEARDROPS ON MY GUITAR

SEE PAGE 14.

A PLACE IN THIS WORLD

WRITERS Taylor Swift, Robert Ellis Orrall, Angelo Petraglia

—

Written when Taylor was 13 years old as she was trying to find her feet in Nashville, 'A Place in This World' was crafted with skill and dedication, and is loaded with catchy melodies. Listen out for her spiralling vocals in the verses, the layers of chunky guitars and the rise and fall of the arrangement, if you need proof. The lyrics may be a little unsophisticated by the composer's modern standards, based as they are on the idea of being a) a girl and b) alone, but they obviously point to the more muscular direction to follow – and anyway, what songs were you and I writing when we were 13?

Album Artwork: Big Machine Records. Images: Getty Images. *Source: *Billboard* 200, correct as of 2 May 2024.

TOP Taylor with Tim McGraw on stage in 2011.
MIDDLE Several debut songs have featured as Eras surprise songs.
BOTTOM With Liz Rose at the 2010 BMI Country Awards.

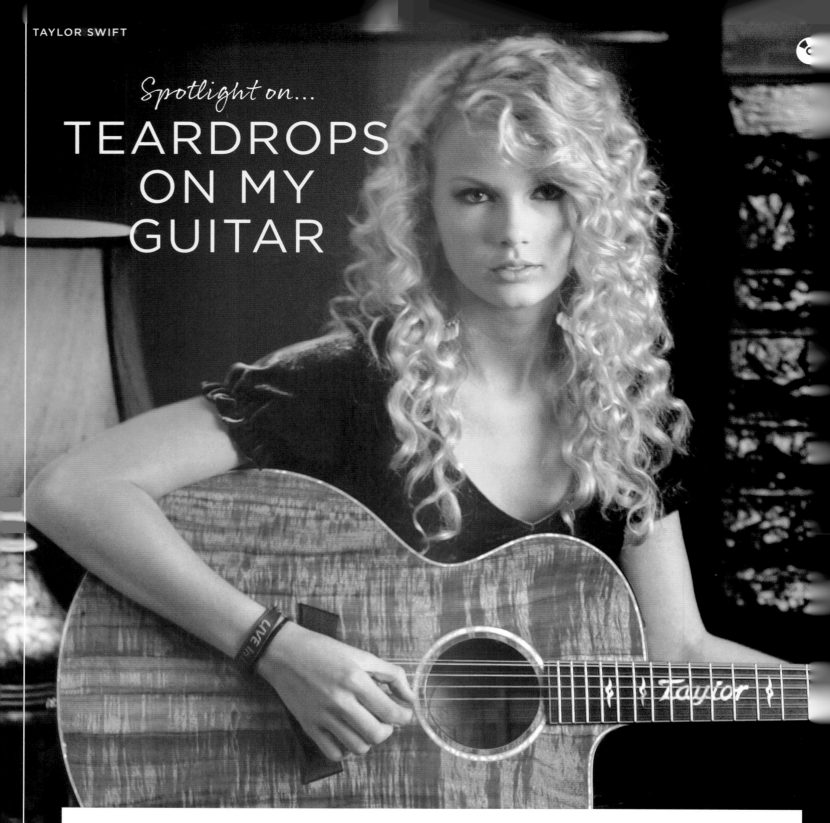

Spotlight on...

TEARDROPS ON MY GUITAR

WRITERS Taylor Swift, Liz Rose

——

Yikes! Who'd want to be Andrew Hardwick, the former high school classmate and confidante of Taylor Swift? As the famous story goes, Hardwick used to sit next to her and drone on about how much he loved his girlfriend while the future superstar nodded politely, never revealing that she was head over heels in love with him. Instead, she wrote this song about him, wisely only identifying him as 'Drew' in the lyrics. Taylor later revealed that he turned up at her house a couple of years after the song became the third single from her debut

album. Having moved on from him since then, she chuckled "Wow, you're late…" and that was it for Drew.

It's a great story, and a charming song too, with the timeless theme of unrequited love. Along acoustic ballad lines like 'Tim McGraw' – and the first Taylor Swift song that you could reasonably call a pop song with country elements rather than a country track – 'Teardrops on My Guitar' tells the tale of a high school crush in convincing, unhurried style. It reached high positions in no fewer than 11 North American chart categories, and even snuck into the upper reaches of the UK charts when it was released there later in 2009.

COLD AS YOU

WRITERS Taylor Swift, Liz Rose
—

Track fives are now renowned for being Taylor's most emotional and vulnerable songs on each album, and that tradition began right here. 'Cold as You' was actually her favourite song on the record, with some of the best lyrics she and Liz Rose had written together. As country as you like, with skirling guitar and violins, this song makes the best of Taylor's higher vocal register, territory that we haven't heard much of in the last decade or so as her voice has matured. Addressing someone who is, as the title implies, emotionally unavailable, 'Cold as You' is pretty much the perfect beefed-up country ballad.

STAY BEAUTIFUL

WRITERS Taylor Swift, Liz Rose
—

It speaks volumes about the quality of the songs on this album that almost any of them could have been released as a single. In particular, 'Stay Beautiful' would have been a contender for radio and TV rotation, offering us a slinky, Beatles-alike vibe loaded with earworm hooks. The topline melody of the verses is so memorable that once you hear it, you won't shift it for hours. As with so many other songs on *Taylor Swift*, it's a cheery pop tune laden with country touches, like a cake adorned with violin-and-banjo icing, an image that we use advisedly because as tunes go, this one is seriously sweet.

> *A full string section lends pathos and depth…*
> *Songs as emotionally powerful as 'Tied Together*
> *with a Smile' don't come along every day*

THE OUTSIDE

WRITERS Taylor Swift
—

One of Taylor's earliest compositions – written when she was just 12 years old – 'The Outside' is a rare example of a musically cheerful song with heart-wrenching lyrics. It was inspired by her experiences of being unpopular at school, and as a result the school classmates who were less than friendly to Taylor back in the Nineties and early Noughties must feel completely humiliated every time they hear it. The vibe is a bit like the theme tune to a teenage drama, appropriately enough, and there might just be a touch of bitterness audible now and then, in particular when it ends on a sudden off-beat.

SHOULD'VE SAID NO

WRITERS Taylor Swift
—

The fifth and last single from this album was also its most uncompromising – a reprimand to some unfaithful and/or untrustworthy lover that tells him exactly where he went wrong. As Taylor told *Great American Family*, it was "a moral statement. It's an 'I love you, we were awesome and great together, but you messed this up and I would still be with you' kinda thing. You said yes, and you should've said no." This US Hot Country chart-topper was also the most rocking song on the album, with squealing electric guitars alternating between the usual acoustic and banjo.

TIED TOGETHER WITH A SMILE

WRITERS Taylor Swift, Liz Rose
—

'Tied Together with a Smile' is a gentle ballad inspired by a friend who was popular at school, but was struggling with an eating disorder. Musically, though, we're in phones-aloft mode: you can imagine this song uniting a stadium with its big old chorus and plenty of heartstring-twanging sentiments. A full string section lends pathos and depth, there are oodles of expert vocal harmonies, and there's a fully leaded ascent towards each chorus that will have you dashing a tear from your eye, you mark our words. Songs as emotionally powerful as this don't come along every day.

MARY'S SONG (OH MY MY MY)

WRITERS Taylor Swift, Liz Rose, Brian Maher
—

How could Taylor Swift be such a master of nostalgia at the age of 16? This sweet, uplifting slice of romance is a guitar-heavy tale, not merely of a youthful love affair, but of a lifelong marriage that lasts until the characters in the lyrics are 87 and 89 years old. Not the usual teenage subject matter, then, but it works perfectly, right up until its wistful final chord. Check out the descending chord sequence in the chorus, always a reliable songwriting trick if you want to switch on the bittersweet emotions. The maturity in this song is almost uncanny: it sounds like the work of a much more seasoned writer.

Spotlight on...
OUR SONG

WRITERS Taylor Swift

The standard edition of the *Taylor Swift* album ends with this sassy composition, in which Taylor half-raps, half-sings the verse lyrics before the chorus, a tongue-twisting sequence of syllables overlaying a set of cheerful, ascending chords. It was released as the album's third single but sits perfectly as the final song on the album itself, summing up the LP's generally mellow vibe.

It reached the top of the US Hot Country Songs chart and stayed there for six weeks, in doing so making Taylor the youngest ever person to top that list with a self-penned, self-sung composition. The song also reached No.16 on the main *Billboard* singles chart, went platinum in Canada and then achieved an amazing quadruple-platinum status in the US.

What made this song such a success? Simple – its easy-to-love, finger-clickable sound and the expertly crafted lyrics. Here, Taylor told the story of a car ride with her boyfriend, who points out that the couple don't have a song, as in a track that is special to them both. She explains that their memories together form their song, a nice analogy that is completely relatable.

I'M ONLY ME WHEN I'M WITH YOU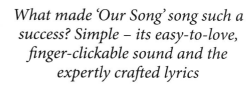

WRITERS Taylor Swift, Robert Ellis Orrall, Angelo Petraglia
—

The first of the three bonus cuts on the deluxe edition of the *Taylor Swift* album has a very different flavour to the easy guitar fare of the other songs. It's a pop-rock song aimed at the dancefloor, loaded with Bruce Springsteen-type escape-from-it-all sentiments ("A small-town boy and girl living in a crazy world"), with only a hoedown violin solo revealing its country roots. We'll go so far as to state that this song points directly to the stylistic variations that Taylor would embrace a couple of albums down the road, even if actual synths and sequencers were still over the horizon at this point.

> *What made 'Our Song' song such a success? Simple – its easy-to-love, finger-clickable sound and the expertly crafted lyrics*

INVISIBLE

WRITERS Taylor Swift, Robert Ellis Orrall
—

This cute, heartfelt ballad of unrequited love sees Taylor informing the object of her affection that his other half will never see him as she, the song's narrator, does. As with all the best love songs, the instrumentation is subtle and stripped-down, focusing on Taylor's higher-than-usual warbling with only an understated piano and strings to keep her company. After a slow build, there's a step down at the end to let the emotions subside, and the song ends on the whine of a slide guitar. It's an object lesson in keeping the music from overwhelming the words and sentiment.

A PERFECTLY GOOD HEART

WRITERS Taylor Swift, Brett James, Troy Verges
—

Addressing a lover who has dumped her – and broken her 'perfectly good heart' in doing so – Taylor organises her thoughts on the subject in fine style on this convincing final track. As with 'Invisible', she keeps the music in service to the message, asking how she can return to her former, happy state – and who doesn't relate to that question? In many ways this song sums up the overall theme of the album: the ending of relationships, and why it has to hurt so much when they happen. A perfect country music theme, of course, but also a universal one.

TOP Pictured with Scott Borchetta, who signed Taylor to his label Big Machine Records in 2005.
MIDDLE Posing with her very first industry award back in 2007.
BOTTOM Taylor toured with other artists to promote her debut.

Taylor Swift
Taylor's Version

COMING SOON...

Taylor occasionally plays her early songs in the Eras Acoustic set.

Image. Getty Images.

ALBUM 02

⟶✦

11 NOV 2008

Taylor's Version
ALBUM 01

✦⟵

09 APR 2021

FEARLESS

13 WEEKS AT NO.1*

Taylor's stratospheric second album proved that if you want to find your Prince Charming, you've got to kiss a few frogs…

WORDS BY HENRY YATES

FEARLESS

WRITERS Taylor Swift, Liz Rose, Hillary Lindsey

—

Kicking off her make-or-break second album, the ethereal opening chimes of 'Fearless' evoked the shivers and butterflies of a first date (in fact, Taylor admitted, the relationship in the song was theoretical, as she wasn't even "in the beginning states of dating anybody"). Co-written with Liz Rose and Hillary Lindsey – with Nathan Chapman keeping the production crystal-clean – it was also the perfect encapsulation of Taylor's headspace as she teetered on the brink of megastardom. "Fearless doesn't mean you're completely unafraid and it doesn't mean that you're bulletproof," she explained. "It means that you have a lot of fears, but you jump anyway."

FIFTEEN

WRITERS Taylor Swift

—

Taylor's songwriting antennae went up as she stepped through the doors of Hendersonville High School in the mid-Noughties, and a few years later this coming-of-age strum bottled the dates, daydreams and dashed hopes of those formative years. Arguably, 'Fifteen' belongs most to her real-life best friend, Abigail Anderson, who is namechecked and remembered for giving "everything she had to a boy who changed his mind". Including such a personal lyric, the singer reflected, was an agonising decision – and even with Anderson's blessing, Taylor admitted that recording the song brought her to tears.

Spotlight on...

LOVE STORY

SEE PAGE 22.

HEY STEPHEN

WRITERS Taylor Swift

—

While Taylor's claws would come out as she flamed ex-lovers on later albums, 'Hey Stephen' is perhaps the sweetest shout-out to a crush in her catalogue. She's joked about the song's subject – from Stephen King to Stephen Colbert – but the true inspiration was Stephen Barker Liles of country duo Love and Theft, who was so touched by the dedication that he returned the favour on 2011's answer song 'Try to Make It Anyway'. "It's actually one of the nicest things anybody's ever done for me," he said.

Album Artwork: Republic Records. Images: Getty Images. *Source: *Billboard* 200, 2 May 2024, original and TV combined.

TOP With best friend Abigail Anderson, who inspired 'Fifteen'.
MIDDLE The Fearless Tour was Taylor's first headline show.
BOTTOM Taylor's haul of four Grammys at the 2010 awards.

Spotlight on...
LOVE STORY

WRITERS Taylor Swift

Taylor had been consumed by *Romeo and Juliet* as a young teenager – but when she brought home an early suitor to blanket disapproval, she found herself living the Montague-versus-Capulet narrative. "He was a creep but I, at the time, just thought he was amazing," she told *CBS News*. After the pre-chorus line "You were Romeo, you were throwing pebbles and my daddy said 'Stay away from Juliet'" came to mind, Taylor sketched out the rest of the song in just 20 minutes flat on her bedroom floor. In her version, she sweetened Shakespeare's tale of star-crossed lovers, rewriting the original tragedy to give her Romeo and Juliet a happily ever after.

Taylor convinced her dubious inner circle that 'Love Story' was a hit, she would be proved right. This breakthrough single topped various charts in Australia, Canada, the US and Japan, and found itself comfortably in the Top 10 around the world. Some 18 million global sales later, it's a stone-cold signature Swift tune.

WHITE HORSE

WRITERS Taylor Swift, Liz Rose

—

Written just weeks after 'Love Story' – with Taylor penning the first verse solo and co-writer Liz Rose helping her to flesh out the rest – 'White Horse' was a companion piece representing the flipside of the fairytale, where it's not all happily ever after. "It's about that moment where you realise the person you thought was going to be Prince Charming and sweep you off your feet is really not going to sweep you off your feet," Taylor told *MTV News*. "You realise that person isn't your future, they're your past."

Spotlight on...

YOU BELONG WITH ME

SEE PAGE 29.

BREATHE (FEAT. COLBIE CAILLAT)

WRITERS Taylor Swift, Colbie Caillat

—

MySpace phenom Colbie Caillat had already left her mark on *Fearless*, with album mixer Justin Niebank citing the singer's debut record *Coco* – and especially 'Bubbly' – as a touchstone for its "honesty and commitment to keeping the arrangements simple". But Caillat's involvement became more tangible when Taylor caught up with her for a quickfire Nashville writing session that yielded 'Breathe' in half an hour. The original soared, but Caillat was happy to revisit her vocal for *Fearless (Taylor's Version)*. "I think my voice has gotten stronger," she told *The Zak Kuhn Show*. "When I listen back, I'm like, 'Oh my God, you sound like a baby…'"

TELL ME WHY

WRITERS Taylor Swift, Liz Rose

—

Liz Rose was one of a handful of confidants for whom young Taylor let her guard down – and the carefree sunshine of the 'Tell Me Why' chord sequence conceals some of her most biting lyrics. "I walked into Liz's house [after a breakup]," she told *Associated Press*. "She goes, 'If you could say everything you were thinking to him right now, what would you start with?' I just started rambling, and she was writing down everything that I was saying, and so we turned it into a song."

TOP A portrait from the BMI Country Awards in 2009.
MIDDLE With 'Breathe' collaborator Colbie Caillat.
BOTTOM On stage in Sydney, Australia, during the Fearless Tour.

LEFT Taylor with her mum, Andrea, for whom she wrote 'The Best Day'.
RIGHT Performing 'Forever & Always' at the 2009 CMA Awards.

YOU'RE NOT SORRY

WRITERS Taylor Swift

—

Fearless is an album full of supposed Prince Charmings revealed as cheating frogs, and this angsty piano power-ballad saw Taylor call time on an ex's destructive cycle of abuse and apology. "The songs that I write by myself are special to me," she explained, "Because usually I write them so fast that I write them in the moment, when that song has been inspired by something that just happened. I wrote 'You're Not Sorry' about a guy who kept apologising and kept doing the same thing again and again."

FOREVER & ALWAYS

WRITERS Taylor Swift

—

With a day to spare, Taylor begged label boss Scott Borchetta to let her include this late addition to the *Fearless* tracklisting. Smart move: *Pitchfork* ranked 'Forever & Always' as the album's best song, and while the original take has a chippy strut, the album's *Platinum Edition* (and later the 2021 re-recording) also includes an alternate rendition stripped back to piano and cello. "The original version seems frustrated, angry and confused," Taylor explained, "But this version of the song is just really sad."

THE WAY I LOVED YOU

WRITERS Taylor Swift, John Rich

—

The big twist of this track is that the idealised man she is seeing leaves Taylor missing the furniture-trashing fights and rain-soaked passion she had with a fiery former beau. Along with 'Hey Stephen', this song employs what would become a recurring romantic motif across Taylor's discography: kissing in the rain. Writing alongside John Rich (bassist of classic country band Lonestar) made the song real, she told *That's Country*: "He was able to relate to it because he is that complicated, frustrating, messy guy in his relationships."

THE BEST DAY

WRITERS Taylor Swift

—

As a thank you for her mother Andrea's support in the hardscrabble early years, Taylor spent snatched moments in the *Fearless* sessions working on a secret tribute track. When the singer finally presented 'The Best Day' to her parents on Christmas Eve, there wasn't a dry eye in the Swift house. "She had made this edited music video," Andrea told *NBC News*. "I'm looking on the TV and this video comes up with this voice that sounds exactly like Taylor's. And I looked over at her and she said, 'I wrote it for you, Mom'. That's when I lost it."

> *'The Way I Loved You' employs what would become a recurring romantic motif across Taylor's discography: kissing in the rain*

On the red carpet
at the 2009
CMA Awards in
Nashville.

CHANGE

WRITERS Taylor Swift

—

Having signed to Big Machine Records – at that point a minnow amongst the giants of the Nashville music scene – Taylor wrote this "underdog story" to pump up her own self-belief and convince herself she had a "fighting chance" of success. But the lyrical pep-talk of 'Change' struck a wider chord, with this revvy rocker used as a theme for the 2008 Olympics and featured on the *AT&T Team USA Soundtrack* compilation. Perhaps Taylor can take some credit for the States winning the most medals (112) at that summer's event?

JUMP THEN FALL

WRITERS Taylor Swift

—

A bonus track for the *Fearless: Platinum Edition*, 'Jump Then Fall' was unashamedly upbeat, with Taylor telling *MTV News* that "It's really bouncy and happy and lovey, with this really cool banjo part". The song explores the thrill of becoming enamoured with someone and hoping that they feel the same way too, as she secretly wills him to fall for her. If you're looking for the perfect scenario for playing it, she added in another interview, wait for a sunny day and roll the car windows down: "It's the happiest, danciest song to drive down the street listening to."

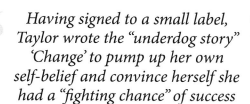

> " *Having signed to a small label, Taylor wrote the "underdog story" 'Change' to pump up her own self-belief and convince herself she had a "fighting chance" of success* "

UNTOUCHABLE

WRITERS Cary Barlowe, Nathan Barlowe, Tommy Lee James, Taylor Swift

—

When Taylor was asked to perform a cover on TV show *Stripped*, Nathan Barlowe of Nashville rockers Luna Halo recalled, she "could have chosen any song in the world". But she decided on Barlowe's cult gem from 2007, reworking 'Untouchable' for the performance, and adding a studio take to expanded releases of *Fearless*. Barlowe thought Taylor's new version was "amazing", he told *The Tennessean*, "It caught me off guard because I didn't even recognize the melody of the verse and some of the arrangement."

TOP With her backing singers during the Eras *Fearless* set.
MIDDLE On stage at Madison Square Garden on the Fearless Tour.
BOTTOM At a benefit for the Country Music Hall of Fame in 2009.

02   FEARLESS   01   TAYLOR SWIFT   02

► 13   ►   ► 13   ►

LEFT Fairytale-themed outfits were a common sight during Taylor's early eras.
RIGHT The Eras Tour's second set includes plenty of joyful *Fearless* throwbacks.

COME IN WITH THE RAIN ⭐

WRITERS Taylor Swift, Liz Rose

'Come in with the Rain' had been up Taylor's sleeve for years – the song is date-stamped to 2006, with early mixes surfacing on MySpace even before her debut album – but this twelve-string jangler finally saw official light of day on the *Fearless: Platinum Edition*. Fan theorists believe the lyric is about her high school boyfriend Sam Armstrong, but the track clearly still has resonance for thirty-something Taylor; she played it as a surprise song in Tokyo on The Eras Tour, revealing: "I'm pretty sure I've never performed this one live!"

THE OTHER SIDE OF THE DOOR ⭐

WRITERS Taylor Swift

A deep cut that has so far had two unexpected airings during The Eras Tour – as a surprise song in Atlanta and a mash-up in Australia – 'The Other Side of the Door' celebrates the flying sparks missing from the relationship in 'The Way I Loved You'. "It talks about when you're in a fight with somebody and you slam the door and you're like, 'Leave me alone, don't talk to me, I hate you!'" Taylor explained. "But what you really mean is, 'Please go buy me flowers and beg that I forgive you and stand at the door and don't leave for three days.'"

SUPERSTAR ⭐

WRITERS Taylor Swift

Taylor and her early collaborator Liz Rose struck gold again on this yearning ballad, whose role-reverse lyric sees Swift gazing up adoringly at the object of her desires on the stage. It combines themes that Taylor has explored across her career: infatuation, fame, and feeling invisible. Many Swifties speculated that the superstar in question was country singer Jake Owen (who Taylor opened a show for back in 2006), but given the song's hidden message in the album's liner notes – "I'll never tell" – this one is likely to stay a mystery.

TODAY WAS A FAIRYTALE 💿

WRITERS Taylor Swift

Making her big-screen debut in 2010's *Valentine's Day*, Taylor also handed producers this mandolin-trilling ode to a dream date for the movie's soundtrack. While the film itself was a flop, the song was a milestone for Taylor when it was released as a single – it was downloaded from iTunes almost 100,000 times on its day of release and pushing her career digital sales past 25 million. It originally reached No.2 on the *Billboard* Hot 100, and was later included on the *Fearless (Taylor's Version)* release.

> '*Superstar*' *combines themes that Taylor has explored across her career: infatuation, fame, and feeling invisible*

Spotlight on...
OU BELONG WITH ME

WRITERS Taylor Swift, Liz Rose

Even as a teenage songwriter, Taylor was always 'on' – so when she overheard a fraught phone call between a bandmate and his girlfriend, she penned the first line of 'You Belong with Me'. With that spark of inspiration, she started drafting a narrative about a boy tugged between a "girl next door" and a "snobby, ridiculous, overrated girl".

Driven by a country-pop guitar chug, the lyric was irresistible to anyone who had experienced the battlelines of high school cliques and the turmoil of unrequited love. But it was director Roman White's video that sent 'You Belong with Me' over the top, with Taylor playing both the loveable dork and snooty queen bee.

"'You Belong with Me' is a song that just absolutely changed my life," she reflected of the US No.2 hit in a 2021 interview with iHeartRadio. "I never would have imagined how many people I would see in a crowd one day screaming, 'She wears short skirts, I wear T-shirts…', or there would be think pieces about it or that it would be this thing that launched me and my career into this place that I never imagined it would go to."

Taylor started making her 'heart hands' gesture in the *Fearless* days.

YOU ALL OVER ME (FEAT. MAREN MORRIS)

WRITERS Taylor Swift, Scooter Carusoe

—

With the 2021 release of *Fearless (Taylor's Version)*, anyone who felt Swift had strayed too far from her roots got a hit of nostalgia from this straight-up country ballad, praised by *NME* as "a time capsule of the *Fearless* era" (and featuring Texan country star Maren Morris on backing vocals). "I remember us painstakingly trying to come up with all these different symbolic imagery references to how it could feel after you have your heart broken," Taylor said of 2005 writing sessions with Scooter Carusoe. "I think one of the hardest things about heartbreak is feeling like you carry that damage with you."

THAT'S WHEN (FEAT. KEITH URBAN)

WRITERS Taylor Swift, Brad Warren, Brett Warren

—

Nashville's sibling songwriters Brad and Brett Warren were understandably taken aback when Taylor called to announce she was re-recording the song they'd co-written together 17 years earlier ("I'll never forget the first thing they said – 'Well, I think that's the longest hold we've ever had!'" she recalled). Just as unlikely, Keith Urban was at a mall in Australia doing his Christmas shopping when he was offered the second verse. "So I'm sitting in the food court," the singer told Ellen DeGeneres, "It was an unusual place to be hearing unreleased Taylor Swift music."

> *Taylor explained her rationale for cutting back the original* Fearless *tracklisting: 'Don't want too many breakup songs, don't want too many down-tempo songs, can't fit that many songs on a physical ed…'*

MR. PERFECTLY FINE

WRITERS Taylor Swift

—

For whatever reason, this sad-but-savage takedown of a "casually cruel" ex was left off the original 2008 album, but thankfully got its chance to shine on the 2021 re-recording. "It was definitely an early indicator of me creeping towards a pop sensibility," Taylor said of the glistening Laurel Canyon sound that evoked *Rumours*-era Fleetwood Mac. "I really love the bridge – I think the lyrics are just wonderfully scathing and full of the teen angst you would hope to hear on an album that I wrote when I was 17 or 18."

DON'T YOU

WRITERS Taylor Swift, Tommy Lee James

—

After a pulsing psychedelic intro with shades of The Beatles' 'Strawberry Fields Forever', 'Don't You' mellowed into a desolate synth ballad that captured the wrench of letting a lover go. It tackles the conflicting emotions of wanting to move on, but still being in love with an ex and finding it too painful to stay friends. "You know, your life is kind of in shambles and they've moved on and they're really happy," Taylor told Spotify, "And it's almost, like, even them being nice to you hurts you."

WE WERE HAPPY

WRITERS Taylor Swift, Liz Rose

—

When announcing the Taylor's Version, Swift explained her rationale for cutting back the original *Fearless* tracklisting: "Don't want too many breakup songs, don't want too many down-tempo songs, can't fit that many songs on a physical ed…" she clarified. That's surely why we had to wait until 2021 to hear this bruised exploration of a young love turned to dust. By the time of the re-recording sessions, Taylor's contacts book had grown significantly, allowing her bring in A-list guests Keith Urban (on harmonies) and The National's Aaron Dessner (on guitar, bass and keys).

BYE BYE BABY

WRITERS Taylor Swift, Liz Rose

—

Originally titled 'The One Thing' – but retitled and rewritten after dropping out of contention for the original *Fearless* – 'Bye Bye Baby' was a stellar example of Taylor's songwriting telepathy with Liz Rose. It's far from a Hollywood ending ("It wasn't just like a movie," she sings over eerie, almost out-of-tune backing, "The rain didn't soak through my clothes down to my skin"). But this story of an unexpected breakup tied the perfect tear-streaked bow on the Taylor's Version tracklisting, and sounded even more powerful from the lips of an artist who by 2021 had been around the block a few times.

ALBUM 03

✦

25 OCT 2010

Taylor's Version
ALBUM 03

✦

07 JUL 2023

SPEAK NOW

8 WEEKS AT
NO. 1*

Taylor's third album explores all the things she wishes she had
said to various people throughout her life

WORDS BY FARRAH FROST

MINE

WRITERS Taylor Swift

—

Speak Now's opening song encapsulates much of what Taylor has become known for: world-building storytelling, specific-yet-universal details, a sense of hopeless romanticism, deft wordplay and a triumphant bridge. Addressed to her partner throughout, we see the relationship build and falter through her eyes, until the bridge flips the perspective on its head and we hear the partner return her affections. It takes us through the relationship journey of a couple who hold onto their love, despite their day-to-day tribulations. This sets the tone for the wistful, full-hearted love Taylor displays throughout the album.

SPARKS FLY

WRITERS Taylor Swift

—

Here, Taylor leaves no descriptive stone unturned, from her lover's eye colour to just how close they stood together. Despite the expanse of emotion covered, the song actually represents a fleeting moment – a theme she revisits in 'Enchanted'. Its central command – to "drop everything now" – propels the song forward into the urgent, unabashed celebration of romance. The track so exemplifies the whole *Speak Now* album; it was this song that she chose to perform as she announced the re-recorded *Speak Now (Taylor's Version)* live in Nashville during The Eras Tour in 2023.

Spotlight on...

BACK TO DECEMBER

SEE PAGE 35.

SPEAK NOW

WRITERS Taylor Swift

—

The title track, 'Speak Now' takes place at the fabled wedding of an ex. According to 2010 interviews, it's inspired by the real-life wedding of a friend's ex-boyfriend. Weddings are a recurring motif in Taylor's songs – understandable for someone who writes about love so frequently – from 'Love Story' through to 'You're Losing Me' and beyond. 'Speak Now' cements Taylor as an optimist and daydreamer, as well as a skilled lyricist. The vivid imagery conjured with pastry-like dresses and shaky hands brings to life a naturally shy girl, an underdog, showing strength and fearlessness in the face of losing her one true love. It also features a well-placed giggle as she indulges in this fantasy alongside us.

TOP On stage during the Speak Now World Tour.
MIDDLE At the 2011 Academy of Country Music Awards.
BOTTOM Performing at the American Music Awards in 2010.

TOP With John Mayer at the Z100 Jingle Ball in 2009.
MIDDLE On stage in Missouri during the Speak Now World Tour.
BOTTOM Selena Gomez joined Taylor on stage in New York.

DEAR JOHN

WRITERS Taylor Swift

——

In the 2023 release of *Speak Now (Taylor's Version)*, Taylor writes in the album prologue that 'Dear John' is her "most scathing" song. It is a letter to an ex detailing her experience of their uneasy relationship. A searing and mournful assessment, Taylor doesn't skimp on the specifics and calls out the misery of a partner who is not reciprocating the love she is tentatively offering. Taylor revisits this theme later in 'tolerate it', on *folklore*. Whether the named 'John' is truly her ex John Mayer, or merely an ode to the wartime artform of separating from your military husband via mail, is for you to decide.

> *Combining reality with imagination and memory recurs throughout this album*

MEAN

WRITERS Taylor Swift

——

The album's most explicitly country track is filled with bluegrass inspiration and led by banjo. It is an anthem for bullying victims everywhere. It skewers her detractors as simply "mean", and predicts their eventual bitterness and her growth beyond the reach of their negativity. When performed live, Taylor often takes a comic pause after the line criticising her singing. This defiant moment gives her critics a moment to consider their folly, and highlights a bizarre insult to one of the world's most accomplished artists. The *Speak Now* album prologue is Taylor's first admission of her vocal training, possibly motivated by the comments identified in the song.

THE STORY OF US

WRITERS Taylor Swift

——

Literary references are favourite devices of Taylor's. 'The Story of Us' is scattered with "endings" and "pages" and "tragedy", and she propels us into the second half of the song with "Next chapter!" The track takes us back and forth between the lived experience of being in a crowded room with an ex, and fantasising about their relationship internally. Combining reality with imagination and memory recurs throughout this record, as in 'Back to December', 'Speak Now' and 'I Can See You'. The result is an album with the vivid feel of taking place inside the mind of a 20-year-old romantic.

Spotlight on...
BACK TO DECEMBER

WRITERS Taylor Swift

A breath away from the riveting romances of *Speak Now*, here Taylor takes an inward look at a lost love. Apologies are a common theme in her catalogue, but they most often are from the imagined perspective of the love interest in question, as in 'betty', 'How You Get the Girl', and 'You're Not Sorry'. It's this theme of regret that gives the song an air of maturity as Taylor explores this self-inflicted heartbreak.

Wistful, Taylor revisits key moments of the relationship breakdown with her typical balance of precision and ubiquity. Her trademark ability to find universality in the most specific of details is on full display here: you are never quite sure whether the roses that were left to wilt are real or metaphorical. Equally affecting, in both the original 2010 recording and the 2023 re-release, her vocal delivery deliberately lets a youthful voice slip through the power ballad's veneer to layer on the naïvety of her mistakes.

Confirmed to have been inspired by her relationship with Taylor Lautner (as revealed by Lautner himself), the couple repaired their relationship and remain close friends. What's more, Lautner later featured on *Speak Now (Taylor's Version)* in the form of a starring role in the 'I Can See You' music video.

On stage during the
Speak Now World
Tour at Madison
Square Garden.

NEVER GROW UP

WRITERS Taylor Swift

—

The melancholic, sweet 'Never Grow Up' is almost like a lullaby to Taylor's younger self, though she has since dedicated the song to the children of her friends. It was also a message to her young fans, as Taylor explained: "Every once in a while I look [at the crowd] and I see a little girl who is seven or eight, and I wish I could tell her all of this." The central message of the song is one of keeping your youthful innocence and relishing the joys of your childhood. The lyrics demonstrate a different kind of maturity from Taylor. She offers advice on cherishing moments in this love letter to her family experiences. It's one of a handful of songs Taylor has written about familial love – in good company with 'The Best Day' and 'marjorie'.

INNOCENT

WRITERS Taylor Swift

—

This was the first musical acknowledgement Taylor made of her experience with Kanye West infamously storming the stage at the 2009 MTV Video Music Awards, but it would not be the last song about him. Here, she is pensive but ultimately forgiving, assigning the then "32 and still growing up" West a youthful naïvety. In her prologue message for the 2023 re-recording, Taylor reflected: "Some expected anger and instead got compassion and empathy with 'Innocent'". In addition to the widely presumed references to Kanye, there are also some fan theories that Taylor draws inspiration from previous romantic relationships for this song, or that it can be interpreted as more of a message to herself.

> " 'Enchanted' tells us the dreamy story of a
> new fable: meeting your love for the first time "

ENCHANTED

WRITERS Taylor Swift

—

This is Taylor at her most whimsical, fantastical and romantic. We know she's a fan of fairytales from moments across her catalogue – as seen in the *Cinderella*-toned music videos to 'Love Story' and 'Bejeweled' – but 'Enchanted' tells us the dreamy story of a new fable: meeting your love for the first time. The dramatic score and uplifting production offer a triumphant backdrop to the timeless experience of wondering and excitement. The bridge offers a shadow to the song's optimism, as Taylor wrestles with the unknown: does he love someone else? It's a testament to her ability to encapsulate the fullness of even the most nuanced of emotions.

HAUNTED

WRITERS Taylor Swift

—

The orchestral, rock-infused precursor to *reputation*, this song hinges on the moment you realise that your relationship is on a knife-edge, of the feeling that you have lost someone without realising it was happening. *Rolling Stone* magazine reviewed a 2010 performance of 'Haunted' as being "full emo", alluding to the rock opera production and the desperation on display in the lyrics. The song places a tentative step into a more emo genre, and is in retrospect possibly a clue to her collaborations with emo music legends Fall Out Boy and Hayley Williams in the 'From the Vault' tracks, later released on 2023's *Speak Now (Taylor's Version)*.

BETTER THAN REVENGE

WRITERS Taylor Swift

—

Hell hath no fury like Taylor scorned. Angry Taylor in her early albums is driven by a youthful petulance, unlike the measured fury we see in later songs like 'mad woman' and 'my tears ricochet'. Rather, 'Better than Revenge' revels in her anger like a righteous teenager. The result is a fun, rock-tinged track brimming with passion as she admonishes a love rival. The original 2010 recording contained one of her most controversial lyrics – with Taylor quietly swapping the "She's better known for the things that she does on the mattress" lines for the less contentious "He was a moth to the flame, she was holding the matches" metaphor in 2023's *Speak Now (Taylor's Version)*.

LAST KISS

WRITERS Taylor Swift

—

According to Taylor, 'Last Kiss' was the "saddest song" she'd written. It is certainly up there with 'All Too Well' in terms of beloved Swiftie breakup songs. Her heartbreak is on full display in this emotional ballad, as is a potential Easter egg indicating who the song is about: fans speculate the 27-second-long instrumental introduction is a homage to the 27-second phone call her then partner Joe Jonas made to break up with her. The 2010 version includes a particularly tear-inducing shaky breath, which fans were disappointed to discover was not recreated in the re-recorded Taylor's Version, although the timelessness of the description of her devastation remains.

Spotlight on...
LONG LIVE

WRITERS Taylor Swift
—

This triumphant track features many of Taylor's favourite techniques and imagery: the fairytale invoked by fighting dragons, the royalty references with crowns swapped for caps, the American high school backdrop of wearing torn jeans and being handed trophies. It also has that Swiftian knack of making a specific experience – her standing on stage with bandmates in front of a crowd – and casts it in such a universally relatable light that it could be about any great accomplishment of the listeners. Addressing her bandmates, Taylor shares her amazement and pride at their collective achievements. Like all great anthems, the production soars and instils a celebratory, jubilant mood to this story of an unlikely hero achieving their dreams – no matter how 'absurd'.

Swiftie lore states that Taylor was so uncertain about the success of this self-written album that she issues 'Long Live' as a pre-emptive "thank you and goodbye" to her fans as the finale track to the original album. She needn't have worried: the song is now a tribute to the unending and extraordinary relationship Taylor has with Swifties, it featured in several of her world tour setlists, and was the closing credits track to *The Eras Tour* concert film. The crowds indeed go wild.

OURS

WRITERS Taylor Swift

—

A sweet song that professes a love that endures the tribulations any relationship might face: judgement, being apart, ex-partners who might jump out at you. Despite it all, Taylor finds love and security in her partner. Being judged for her relationships, and the impact an outsider's input can have, is a rich source of inspiration for Taylor, with the theme explored in 'I Know Places' and 'But Daddy I Love Him', for example. On a sadder note, the song title is possibly referenced ten years later in *evermore*'s 'champagne problems' when Taylor implies she and her partner won't say "that word" again.

SUPERMAN

WRITERS Taylor Swift

—

It's speculated that 'Superman' was inspired by Taylor's relationship with John Mayer. The production is upbeat – the lyrics, however, are open to multiple readings. They can either be viewed as an overall compliment to the 'Superman', or instead portray an anxious Taylor, marooned at home alone, not receiving cards or flowers, as she comforts herself about the importance of his work and reassures him that she'll be waiting. How you view it is up to you, but it is a classic Taylor move to leave such a wide room for interpretation. She is also known to hide sorrowful narratives beneath a cheery track – another notable example being 'Forever Winter'.

> " *Being judged for her relationships is a rich source of inspiration for Taylor* "

ELECTRIC TOUCH
(FEAT. FALL OUT BOY)

WRITERS Taylor Swift

—

The mid-to-late 2000s were dominated by emo rock music, so it's no surprise that Taylor had revealed Fall Out Boy's impact on her songwriting in interviews. Comparisons can certainly be made between Taylor and the band's wordplay and densely packed lyrics. So, when the re-recorded *Speak Now (Taylor's Version)* released 'Electric Touch' from the Vault, it seemed as inevitable as it was unexpected. The song centres on the potential outcomes of a new relationship and the uncertainty that comes with new beginnings. It features one of *Speak Now*'s strongest vocal deliveries, and a trademark falsetto from Fall Out Boy frontman Patrick Stump.

TOP Performing at the Academy of Country Music Awards in 2011.
MIDDLE At the Grammy Awards in Los Angeles, 2010.
BOTTOM During the *Speak Now* chapter of The Eras Tour.

WHEN EMMA FALLS IN LOVE 🔒

WRITERS Taylor Swift

One of three tracks produced by collaborator Aaron Dessener on *Speak Now (Taylor's Version)*, 'When Emma Falls in Love' is a platonic love letter to the mysterious friend Emma. The titular character is observed falling in and out of love through Taylor's admiring eyes. The sprinkling piano has echoes of Train's 'Drops of Jupiter', and the lyrics contain some of the most concise yet descriptive lines of the album – among them the image of a small-town Cleopatra. Yet, as with much of Taylor's work, the reception has largely been driven by speculation on the identity of the Emma in question, with many fans believing it to be the actress Emma Stone.

FOOLISH ONE 🔒

WRITERS Taylor Swift

'Foolish One' takes the almost maternal role of advising the protagonist on the futility of her hope for a doomed relationship. The soft, chiding nature of the chorus gives us the sense that this is in fact Taylor wistfully advising a younger, more naïve version of herself. Naïvety comes up frequently in her self-assessments (in 'Fifteen', for example), perhaps the downside to being a self-confessed hopeless romantic. The advice she doles out neatly suits any one-sided or complicated relationship, or "situationship", once again a great example of Taylor turning her own experiences into a universally relatable message.

> " *Naïvety comes up frequently in Taylor's self-assessments, perhaps the downside to being a self-confessed hopeless romantic* "

I CAN SEE YOU 🔒

WRITERS Taylor Swift

This song comes as a surprisingly sultry addition to the otherwise wholesome and youthful album, perhaps indicating 2010 Taylor's reluctance to share her sensuality. 'I Can See You' benefits from this departure in tone, becoming the track that caused Taylor to break The Beatles' record for being the only artists to hold Top Ten hits from three different albums simultaneously. The song became the second of the Vault tracks to reach Top Ten positions in charts around the globe. The breathy, darker song centres on the secret desires Taylor harbours for a forbidden love. It connects with the album's themes of fantasy and imagination, albeit with a more lustful undercurrent.

TIMELESS 🔒

WRITERS Taylor Swift

Fate, and the inevitably of love, is a theme Taylor enjoys. We see it again explicitly in 'invisible string', but 'Timeless' instead focuses on a variety of past lives or alternate realities. Inspired by a selection of items Taylor browses in an antiques shop, she envisions a love that overcomes whatever historical obstacles are in their way. The song makes an assumed reference to *Romeo and Juliet*, a clear callback to 'Love Story'. Sweetly, it also pays homage to her grandparents' destiny: they were separated in 1944 due to the Second World War. Closing out the 2023 version of the album, 'Timeless' is arguably one of *Speak Now*'s most quintessentially country songs.

CASTLES CRUMBLING (FEAT. HAYLEY WILLIAMS) 🔒

WRITERS Taylor Swift

The melancholic ballad explores Taylor's hypothetical undoing. Assuming it was originally written at the time of the 2010 album's release, it is an eerily accurate prediction of her 2016 downfall in the general public's opinions and her resulting self-inflicted exile. The more mournful sister song to 'Long Live' draws on the same language of royalty (the palace gates and reigns ending) as it bids a regretful farewell to the glory she once held. This song, alongside 'Long Live', demonstrates how valuable Taylor's reputation has always been to her, a theme we see thoroughly explored in *reputation*, and again referenced throughout *folklore*, *evermore* and *Midnights*.

IF THIS WAS A MOVIE

WRITERS Taylor Swift, Martin Johnson

Originally exclusive to the deluxe edition, this is a perfect example of a *Speak Now* track. A yearning song addressed to her lost love, it is packed with Swiftian motifs – blending memories with fantasy, storytelling and universal relatability, and possibly the most enduring Swift image of all: standing in the rain as an indicator of love. The song actually switched albums during the re-recording project, migrating from *Speak Now* to *Fearless* – a decision that we can reasonably assume was to give *Speak Now (Taylor's Version)* the honour of being entirely self-written. (Upon the 2023 version's release, Taylor wrote: "It's an album I wrote alone about the whims, fantasies, heartaches, dramas and tragedies I lived out as a young woman between 18 and 20.")

'Long Live' was added to the Eras setlist after *Speak Now (Taylor's Version)* was released.

ALBUM 04

Taylor's Version
ALBUM 02

22 OCT 2012

12 NOV 2021

RED

8 WEEKS AT NO. 1*

She promised us a fourth album of "heartbreak and healing, rage and rawness, tragedy and trauma" – and *Red* didn't disappoint

WORDS BY HENRY YATES

STATE OF GRACE

WRITERS Taylor Swift

Taylor's switch-up from country gal to pop chick was loud and clear on *Red*'s opener: a drum-driven arena rocker whose spiralling U2-style echo riffs and wide-eyed lyric evoked the first flutterings of a new relationship (with fans speculating Jake Gyllenhaal was her subject, which also goes for most of the record). "I wrote this song about when you first fall in love with someone, the possibilities, and thinking about the different ways that it could go," the singer told *Good Morning America*. "It sounds like the feeling of falling in love, in an epic way."

> *'Red' expanded Taylor's crossover sound… and began her career-long quest to define the colour of love*

RED

WRITERS Taylor Swift

Boarding a night flight to Nashville in September 2011, Taylor found herself scribbling down her rawest emotions and described the resulting title track as "a real turning point" for her fourth album. The opening banjo pluck saluted her country past, but the singer was painting with a new palette, fusing stadium-sized guitars with subtle electronic vocals, while depicting the rise and fall of a relationship through her lyrical kaleidoscope ("Losing him was blue […] Missing him was dark grey […] But loving him was red"). This song expanded Taylor's crossover sound, leaning further into pop-rock territory, and began her career-long quest to define the colour of love.

TREACHEROUS

WRITERS Taylor Swift, Dan Wilson

Writing with Semisonic's Dan Wilson, Taylor slowed down the tracklisting for *Red*'s first ballad. Don't be fooled by the blissed-out vocal and delicate acoustic guitar: 'Treacherous' is spikier than it sounds, riffing on Taylor's favourite theme of a love affair liable to end in a "fiery, burning wreckage". As she told fans at an acoustic session, it's a song "about when you're falling for someone and you know that it's dangerous, and you know that it could just annihilate you if it were to not work out… but you go for it anyway."

Album Artwork: Republic Records. Images: Getty Images. *Source: *Billboard* 200, 2 May 2024, original and TV combined.

TOP Performing 'State of Grace' on *The X Factor USA*.
MIDDLE At the iHeartRadio Music Festival in 2012.
BOTTOM *Red*'s pop sound still featured country elements.

Spotlight on...
I KNEW YOU WERE TROUBLE

WRITERS Taylor Swift, Max Martin, Shellback

The moment when 'I Knew You Were Trouble' dropped its juddering dubstep chorus was the most radical musical curveball on *Red*, perhaps shocking a few old-school country fans but scoring the rapidly evolving singer thousands more. In fact, despite its zeitgeist-ready styling, Taylor had written the song on a piano, before she asked original producers Max Martin and Shellback to make it sound as "chaotic" as her broken heart felt.

But who is the biting track directed at? While the timeline points to John Mayer, Taylor's comments following a performance at the 2013 BRIT Awards attended by Harry Styles suggested the former One Direction member could also claim ownership. She told *The Sunday Times*: "It's not hard to access that emotion when the person the song is directed at is standing by the side of the stage watching."

Spotlight on...

ALL TOW WELL

SEE PAGE 53.

22

WRITERS Taylor Swift, Max Martin, Shellback

—

As the spiritual sequel to the more wistful 'Fifteen', few songs have caught young adulthood's pinballing emotions like '22' (summed up by the lyric: 'We're happy, free, confused and lonely at the same time'). "I learned a lot of lessons the hard way and 15 was a vulnerable age," Swift told *The Daily Beast* of the seven years that led to this retro-synth banger. "And 22 is a vulnerable age, but you're a little more brave. You're a little more ready to take risks and live with the consequences."

I ALMOST DO

WRITERS Taylor Swift

—

Some fans see 'I Almost Do' as part one of a double-header with 'We Are Never Ever Getting Back Together': the first song extending an olive branch to an ex and wondering if their love could reignite (before the second song tears it all down). "It's about the conflict you feel when you want to take someone back and give it another try, but it's hurt you so deeply that you couldn't bear to go through that again," explained the singer. "And you're almost picking up the phone to call them – but you can't. Writing that song is what I did instead of picking up the phone."

WE ARE NEVER EVER GETTING BACK TOGETHER

WRITERS Taylor Swift, Max Martin, Shellback

—

As *Red*'s lead single, 'We Are Never Ever Getting Back Together' made one of chart history's most audacious leaps, pinging from US No.72 to the top of the *Billboard* Hot 100 in a single week (and marking Swift's first chart-topper on home turf). The earworm chorus fell off her fingers when she picked up a guitar, but it was the candid snark of the spoken-word section (inspired by an ex's friend visiting the studio and recorded as an iPhone voice memo) that chimed with fans whose hearts had also been through the wringer. "I made a song I knew would absolutely drive him crazy when he heard it on the radio," Taylor told *USA Today* of her (unnamed) target.

TOP Performing '22' during The Eras Tour in a *Red*-themed outfit.
MIDDLE Taylor and Ed Sheeren started writing together in 2012.
BOTTOM Her epic ringmaster performance at the 2012 MTV EMAs.

STAY STAY STAY

WRITERS Taylor Swift

By her early twenties, Taylor was under no illusions that adult relationships came with flying sparks – but this breezy mandolin jangler argued that it's worth fighting for your lover – even after you've thrown your phone at them during an argument. "There are moments where you're just so sick of that person, you get into a stupid fight," she explained the *Red (Track by Track)* video. "[But] there's something about it that you can't live without. In the bridge it says: 'I'd like to hang out with you for my whole life'. And I think that's probably the key to finding the one, you just want to hang out with them forever."

SAD BEAUTIFUL TRAGIC

WRITERS Taylor Swift

If you'd been a fly on the wall of Taylor's bus during the Speak Now World Tour of 2011, you'd have seen this minor-key strummer take shape, initially composed on ukelele. "I wanted to tell the story in terms of a cloudy recollection of what went wrong," she told *Billboard* of this often-overlooked ode to a past relationship left on the roadside. "It's kind of the murky grey, looking back on something you can't change or get back." The mentions of pictures in lockets and pocketed notes also appear in the Vault track 'Run' later on the 2021 re-recording.

> " *Taylor had previously covered Britney's 'Lucky', a song that explored the gulf between the glittering promises of fame and its tawdry reality* "

THE LAST TIME
(FEAT. GARY LIGHTBODY)

WRITERS Taylor Swift, Gary Lightbody, Jacknife Lee

Snow Patrol's Gary Lightbody told *Rolling Stone* it took just nine hours to capture the original studio version of 'The Last Time' ("She works really fast"). You'd never guess it, with this moody torch song unfolding at stately pace, carried on stormy pianos and choppy orchestration, with the Northern Irish frontman singing in character as a straying boyfriend begging for another last chance. As Taylor told *NPR*: "My visual for this song is, there's a guy on his knees sitting on the ground outside of a door. And on the other side of the door is his girlfriend, who he keeps on leaving."

THE LUCKY ONE

WRITERS Taylor Swift

Taylor had previously covered Britney Spears' 2000 hit 'Lucky', a semi-biographical song that explored the gulf between the glittering promises of fame and its tawdry reality. Twelve years later, 'The Lucky One' was the younger singer's interpretation of the same topic, following the girl who is "new to town with a made-up name" all the way to the moment her "secrets end up splashed on the news front page". Written on the road in Australia, Taylor said her fears had inspired the track: "I'm pretty much singing about what I'm scared of in that song – ending up caught up in this whole thing and lonely and feeling misunderstood."

HOLY GROUND

WRITERS Taylor Swift

Was Joe Jonas the subject of this rootsy stomper, which acknowledges that even failed relationships can be panned for nuggets of gold? As ever, Taylor wasn't telling, but 'Holy Ground' remains one of *Red*'s most open-hearted moments. "It was about the feeling I got when years had gone by and I finally appreciated a past relationship for what it was – rather than what it didn't end up being," she explained in the *Red (Track by Track)* video interview. "I was sitting there thinking about it after I'd just seen him, and I was like, 'You know what? That was good, having that in my life.'"

EVERYTHING HAS CHANGED
(FEAT. ED SHEERAN)

WRITERS Taylor Swift, Ed Sheeran

You wouldn't guess it from the wistful strum, but 'Everything Has Changed' came from a joyously juvenile moment with her buddy Ed Sheeran at Taylor's Los Angeles home. "Ed comes over and we start writing and I'm like, 'Do you want to see my trampoline?' Like I'm five years old all of a sudden," she told *Nova FM*. "So we're bouncing and I hadn't put my guitar down and I was like, 'By the way, do you like this pre-chorus?' And then we just started writing the song that ended up being on the record."

Performing 'The Lucky One' on the Red Tour in 2013.

A classic red lip has remained a distinctive part of Taylor's look to this day.

LEFT Performing 'Starlight' on the Red Tour in 2013.
RIGHT The Eras' *Red* set features high-energy dance numbers and the extended 'All Too Well'.

STARLIGHT

WRITERS Taylor Swift

———

It's thought that Taylor was dating Conor Kennedy when she wrote this sweet love song. She told *The Wall Street Journal* that the song was inspired by seeing a youthful photo of his legendary grandparents, activist Ethel Kennedy and US Attorney General Robert F Kennedy (who was assassinated in 1968). "I came across this picture of these two kids at a dance back in the late-1940s," she explained. "It immediately made me think of, like, how much fun they must have had that night."

THE MOMENT I KNEW

WRITERS Taylor Swift

———

Of the bonus tracks added to *Red*'s deluxe edition, 'The Moment I Knew' might be the most bleakly honest, inspired by her 21st birthday party that the singer described to *Yahoo! Music* as "the worst experience ever" due to her boyfriend's absence. Based on the timeline – Taylor turned 21 on 13 December 2010 – *Rolling Stone* felt "100% confident" that Gyllenhaal was the no-show, but whoever it was, these feelings are raw and real. "It's the most nakedly confessional song on the album," wrote Chris Willman. "Devastating and unmistakable."

BEGIN AGAIN

WRITERS Taylor Swift

———

This finale to the original *Red* standard edition tracklist felt like the light at the end of an emotional tunnel, with 'Begin Again' finding Taylor picking herself up, dusting herself down and looking to the future. "All of a sudden, you have this epiphany that there's hope, that it starts over, that there's rebirth in that whole horrible crash-and-burn end of a relationship," she told *Yahoo! Music* in a 2012 interview. "I think that's a pretty wonderful moment. And for me that moment inspired 'Begin Again.'"

COME BACK... BE HERE

WRITERS Taylor Swift, Dan Wilson

———

Taylor's punishing work schedule – and tendency to date other prolific showbiz types – means her relationships have often been derailed by diaries that just won't sync, and this sad-eyed acoustic bonus track painted the singer and her lover as two ships that pass in the night. "It's about falling for someone and then they have to go away for work," said Swift. "They're travelling, you're travelling, and you're thinking about them, but you're wondering how it's gonna work when there's so much distance between you."

> *'Begin Again' finds Taylor picking herself up,
> dusting herself down and looking to the future*

GIRL AT HOME

WRITERS Taylor Swift

The immediate chorus hook could have made 'Girl at Home' a fan favourite if Taylor had promoted it to the core *Red* tracklisting. Instead, it's a relative cult gem that was originally only available on the deluxe edition – and that's probably how the subject of the song prefers it, given its tale of a male player putting it about while his partner waits up. Whoever the target may have been, Taylor was not impressed with his antics. "It was about a guy who had a girlfriend," she told *Yahoo! Music*, "And I just felt like it was disgusting that he was flirting with other girls."

NOTHING NEW (FEAT. PHOEBE BRIDGERS)

WRITERS Taylor Swift

By the time it was pulled from the Vault and re-recorded for *Red (Taylor's Version)*, 'Nothing New' was almost a decade old, with the early-twenties singer having written it on a flight across Australia, using an Appalachian dulcimer in tribute to Joni Mitchell. Yet the passing years only gave the lyrics more power, with Taylor and indie-folk singer-songwriter Phoebe Bridgers trading world-weary verses. "It's about being scared of aging," she wrote in her journals, "and things changing and losing what you have."

> " *The passing years only gave 'Nothing New' more power, with Taylor and Phoebe Bridgers trading world-weary verses* "

RONAN

WRITERS Taylor Swift, Maya Thompson

Critics who sniped that Taylor only wrote about her own failed relationships were silenced by the gut-punch of 'Ronan'. Sung from the perspective of Maya Thompson – an Arizona mother who lost her three-year-old son to neuroblastoma – the lyric is so minutely observed that you almost felt you shouldn't be listening ("I remember your bare feet down the hallway, I remember your little laugh"). As such, prior to The Eras Tour, Taylor has only performed 'Ronan' twice: once at a 2012 *Stand Up to Cancer* telethon and again when Thompson attended a 1989 World Tour show.

BABE

WRITERS Taylor Swift, Patrick Monahan

With the *Red* tracklisting signed off, this song – co-written with Pat Monahan from the band Train – became an enviable hand-me-down to country duo Sugarland. Jennifer Nettles and Kristian Bush gladly snapped up 'Babe' for 2018's *Bigger* album ("That is a short list, ladies and gentleman, of people to whom she has said, 'Hey, I have a song, you want to sing it?'" laughed Nettles). But Taylor kept one hand on the song, not only contributing guest vocals but featuring in the Sugarland video as a flame-haired secretary in love with actor Brandon Routh's adulterous boss.

BETTER MAN

WRITERS Taylor Swift

Taylor had so much grade-A material for *Red* that even a stunner like 'Better Man' was surplus to requirements. Cut from the original 2012 tracklisting, she instead gifted the song to her long-standing friends in the country group Little Big Town. It was the perfect vehicle for their cascading vocal harmonies, and became the lead single for their 2017 album *The Breaker*. "We didn't ask why she didn't record the song herself," Kimberly Schlapman from the band told Sirius XM. "We just said, 'Thank you very much, we'll take it.'" Fans finally got to hear Taylor's own rendition when it was included on *Red (Taylor's Version)* in 2021.

MESSAGE IN A BOTTLE

WRITERS Taylor Swift, Max Martin, Shellback

While critics theorised that 'Message in a Bottle' was kept off the *Red* running order due to its similarity with '22', any other artist would have killed for this synth-pop outtake's sugar-rush chorus. The first co-write between Taylor, Max Martin and Shellback explored similar lyrical turf to 'Come Back… Be Here' (with the singer asking her absent boyfriend, "How is it in London today?"), while the title nodded to her songwriting philosophy. "Songs for me are like a message in a bottle," Taylor told *The Daily Beast*. "You send them out to the world and maybe the person who you feel that way about will hear about it someday."

Taylor and Phoebe Bridgers at the 2023 iHeartRadio Music Awards.

LEFT Performing a medley of *Red* tracks on *Dick Clark's New Year's Rockin' Eve* with Ryan Seacrest.

RIGHT Taylor and Ed Sheeran have continued to collaborate on songs from time to time.

I BET YOU THINK ABOUT ME (FEAT. CHRIS STAPLETON)

WRITERS Taylor Swift, Lori McKenna

—

Red offered every kind of breakup song, but as she hunkered down with co-writer Lori McKenna at the latter's Massachusetts home during the Speak Now World Tour, Taylor envisioned 'I Bet You Think About Me' as a whisky-soaked, country-flavoured parting gift ("We wanted to kind of make people laugh with it and for it to be sort of a drinking song," the singer told a Boston radio station). As for Stapleton, he recalled that loaning his roughneck twang was a no-brainer: "They called and I answered."

RUN (FEAT. ED SHEERAN)

WRITERS Taylor Swift, Ed Sheeran

—

Shortly before the trampoline session that birthed 'Everything Has Changed', Swift and Sheeran had joined forces on this delicate escapist ballad. In an interview with *Capital FM* after the Taylor's Version was released in 2021, the British songwriter explained how he was secretly disappointment that 'Run' fell off the original *Red* tracklisting. "It was always my favourite one, but 'Everything Has Changed' just ended up sounding better…" he said. "I've never really wanted to nudge Taylor about it because it's her song and her thing […] I'm so happy it's seeing the light of day."

FOREVER WINTER

WRITERS Taylor Swift, Mark Foster

—

"We kind of just went into it casually, like, let's just jam and just have fun, and something really cool came out of it," remembered co-writer Mark Foster of this underrated Vault track. But 'Forever Winter' was perhaps knottier than its lush pop-rock stylings suggested, with many fans interpreting the lyric as the travails of someone supporting a loved one through mental health issues. Some believe the song to have been inspired either by Taylor's younger brother, Austin, or her late high school friend, Jeff Lang.

THE VERY FIRST NIGHT

WRITERS Taylor Swift, Amund Bjørklund, Espen Lind

—

Norwegian producers Amund Bjørklund and Espen Lind – collectively known as Espionage – brought writing credits including Train's 'Hey, Soul Sister' and Beyoncé's 'Irreplaceable' to their first session with Taylor. Bumped from the original running order, 'The Very First Night' couldn't match the profile of those mega-hits, but it was an upbeat and effervescent end to the extended album, its wistful lyric and pounding beat summing up *Red*'s mission statement. "I want to be deep in my feels," said Taylor, "but I also want to dance…"

 'All Too Well' arguably stands as Taylor's most detailed observation of a breakup's minutiae

Spotlight on...
ALL TOO WELL

WRITERS Taylor Swift, Liz Rose

Two years before work began on *Red*, Taylor had already sketched the bones of this aching strummer, which arguably stands as her most detailed observation of a breakup's minutiae – right down to the lost scarf from a first date, now kept as a memento in a drawer.

As she told *Popdust*, 'All Too Well' started as a venting session at soundcheck: "I was just playing these chords over and over on stage and my band joined in and I went on a rant". But the song had evolved – and sprawled to five-plus minutes – by the time it appeared on the original *Red* album, with Taylor revealing in an interview with *Good Morning America* that plenty more had ended up on the cutting room floor. "It took me a really long time to filter through everything I wanted to put in without it being a ten-minute song, which you can't put on an album," she said.

Of course, that wasn't enough to satisfy the hardcore fans, and when *Red (Taylor's Version)* arrived in 2021, the kiss-off was the full ten-minute version of 'All Too Well' that dialled up the intensity. "It sums up Swift at her absolute best," wrote *Rolling Stone*'s Rob Sheffield.

ALBUM 05

Taylor's Version
ALBUM 04

27 OCT 2014

27 OCT 2023

1989

11 WEEKS AT NO.1*

This groundbreaking album cemented Taylor as a pop icon, featuring some of her biggest hits and most celebrated songwriting

WORDS BY FARRAH FROST

WELCOME TO NEW YORK

WRITERS Taylor Swift, Ryan Tedder

——

Just as the song's protagonist has moved from their small town to be welcomed into the big city, so too does Taylor leave her country era behind for pop music proper. New York is one of her great ongoing love affairs: it represents freedom and opportunity. Prior to *1989*, the city is name-dropped a handful of times in *Red*, but post-*1989* there are frequent references to the Big Apple scattered throughout her catalogue ('Delicate', 'Cornelia Street' and 'coney island' to name a few). In a crisp little bit of foreshadowing, she tells us that the bright lights do not blind her: we wonder if *reputation* Taylor would agree.

Spotlight on...

BLANK SPACE

SEE PAGE 57.

STYLE

WRITERS Taylor Swift, Max Martin, Shellback, Ali Payami

——

Widely believed to be inspired by (and practically named after) Harry Styles, this track charts the pair's on-and-off relationship, comparing them to timeless outfits. It explores the cycle of yearning for and losing a love. The cinematic storytelling begins with Taylor's beau arriving to pick her up in secret. Secrecy is a prominent theme later in *reputation* and *Midnights*, but here it potentially implies the embarrassment associated with reconnecting with an ex. Built on sexual tension (later referenced in the more explicit 'So It Goes...'), Taylor's portrayal as a "good" girl in provocative clothing is almost a balancing act of her public 'America's sweetheart' persona and her own inner desires.

OUT OF THE WOODS

WRITERS Taylor Swift, Jack Antonoff

——

This was reportedly the first time Taylor wrote her lyrics *after* hearing an instrumental first. In a 2014 interview with *USA Today*, she said she sent Jack Antonoff a voice memo with the lyrics within 30 minutes of receiving the track. It's an astonishing speed to have developed such a fulsome portrayal of fragility and anxiety in a relationship. The Polaroid discussed in the opening verse is an interesting line: it is likely the key reference of the album's cover art, and the "screaming colour" sets the track firmly in Taylor territory of defining the colour of love.

TOP Taylor's move to New York was a bit inspiration on the album.
MIDDLE On the red carpet at the 2014 ACM Awards.
BOTTOM Taylor embraced suitably retro outfits in her *1989* era.

LEFT Even a decade later, 'Shake It Off' is still one of Taylor's biggest hits.
RIGHT Performing 'Bad Blood' on The Eras Tour.

ALL YOU HAD TO DO WAS STAY

WRITERS Taylor Swift, Max Martin

In a callback to 'Stay Stay Stay', Taylor tells her indecisive lover that if he wants her back, he simply should have not ended it in the first place. It's at odds with the sexual tension of 'Style', where the cyclical nature of the relationship took on romantic meaning – in this song she is instead positioned akin to a more frustrated 'We Are Never Ever Getting Back Together', albeit less weary and more imperious. The high-pitched "stay" that repeats throughout the song apparently came to Taylor in a dream, and when she woke up she knew she had to work it into a song.

SHAKE IT OFF

WRITERS Taylor Swift, Max Martin, Shellback

This behemoth mega-hit remains one of Taylor's most commercially successful songs to date. An impossibly catchy empowerment anthem equally applicable to hearing rumours about yourself, your ex starting a new relationship, or the perils of global stardom. It was an obvious choice to be the lead single for 1989, the album that confirmed Taylor's transition to full-on pop music – and it has since cemented her status as a pop icon. 'Shake It Off' broke multiple records, took up residency in the Billboard Hot 100 Top Ten for over six months, has been certified Diamond in the US with over 10 million certified units (sales and streaming), and was named one of the best songs of the decade by multiple publications. If she is in fact dancing on her own, we can only assume she means in her own league.

I WISH YOU WOULD

WRITERS Taylor Swift, Jack Antonoff

This was the first track for 1989 that Taylor and Jack Antonoff worked on together, showcasing Taylor's storytelling at its most cinematic. Inspired by classic 80s John Hughes movies, it explores the feelings of recently separated lovers, both wanting to reunite but being too prideful or unsure to make the first move. The "headlights" that pass her allude to an early headlights reference in 'Style', and to the secret hints she left in the album's accompanying notes ("He drove past her street every night"). The song is also set at 2am: we know Taylor loves the nighttime hours for her most dramatic scenes.

BAD BLOOD (FEAT. KENDRICK LAMAR)

WRITERS Taylor Swift, Max Martin, Shellback (and Kendrick Lamar on the remix)

Taylor is renowned for writing about her past romances, but she was quick to confirm that this song's inspiration was a platonic relationship turned sour (allegedly involving Katy Perry and a tour casting feud). She positions herself as someone not to be messed with: the star-studded music video shows her with a squad of celebrity pals as action heroes, training to defeat a treacherous villain (real-life BFF Selena Gomez). 'Bad Blood' is a precursor to Taylor embodying a more vengeful persona in reputation and later songs like 'Vigilante Shit'. The standard album includes her solo version, but for the remixed single release she joined forces with Kendrick Lamar, who added new verses.

Spotlight on...
BLANK SPACE

WRITERS Taylor Swift, Max Martin, Shellback

———

In 'Blank Space', Taylor comes out swinging. Against the backdrop of intense public scrutiny, her love life was tabloid fodder. She was characterised as a manipulative, boy-mad, crazy woman incapable of keeping love because of her intensity and neediness. She satirises this persona and delivers the story as a manic and unreliable narrator. The song begins with entrapping her lover with promises of magic and heaven. She will shapeshift into whoever he wants her to be, before the tables turn and the storms roll in. In the iconic, award-winning music video, as he flees into the distance we see Taylor welcoming in her next victim.

Impossibly catchy, 'Blank Space' is punctuated with Instagram-caption-worthy lines of being a deceptively well-dressed nightmare, or having the ability to tame a bad guy, if only for a few days.

While the song was undeniably commercially successful (second only to juggernaut 'Shake It Off') and critically lauded, the real impact of 'Blank Space' was how it redefined her public persona. Rather than being a passive recipient of intense scrutiny, Taylor turned the tables and regained control of her story. She is self-aware, and she is smart enough to balance profiting from this attention and skewering it to its core. A mastermind.

Taylor's 1989 World Tour was the highest-grossing tour of 2015.

LEFT Performing 'How You Get the Girl' on the 1989 World Tour.
RIGHT Celebrating *1989*'s release with a Times Square show for *Good Morning America*.

WILDEST DREAMS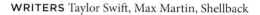

WRITERS Taylor Swift, Max Martin, Shellback

———

Against the backdrop of her own heartbeat (an instrument she reprises in 'You're Losing Me'), Taylor reflects on a relationship's legacy. She can sense its fragility from the very beginning, and she wants to know that her ex will look back with kindness when it is all over. The song is rife with classic Swiftian imagery: nice dresses, burning down loves, redness, escaping together and last kisses. She balances dreamy and whimsical wishes against the pessimistic message of the song: their love is doomed, so she feels nostalgic for it in advance. The song re-emerged on TikTok in 2021, leading to Taylor bringing forward the release of her re-recorded version.

THIS LOVE

WRITERS Taylor Swift

———

This is a dreamy, almost haunting song about a love that ends, begins again, and repeats. Connected to the throughline theme of cyclical relationships on *1989*, 'This Love' is the most poetic and vulnerable. It seems the love washes over her, as the waves invoked in the opening verse, before going back out to sea. Love seemed intrinsically tied up with fate (another recurring theme, as in 'invisible string' or 'Timeless'). According to Taylor, this was the first song written for the album, shortly after *Red* came out. It actually began with the chorus, initially just as a short poem she jotted down in her journal – she then started hearing a melody for it in her head, and the rest is history.

HOW YOU GET THE GIRL

WRITERS Taylor Swift, Max Martin, Shellback

———

Years later, accompanying the song 'betty', Taylor tells us of the great pleasure she takes in writing songs advising men on how to handle their love lives. 'How You Get the Girl' is surely one of those tracks. In this imagined apology, we begin in the rain (the most romantic weather, according to Taylor), and launch into the protagonist's plea; invoking marriage vows and promises to repair the damage he caused by leaving her for six months. Taylor frames the song as an instruction manual for men who don't know how to reignite romance after screwing up a relationship: "It's not gonna be as simple as just sending a text message, like 'Sup? Miss you,' it's not gonna work," she explained on iHeartRadio. "He will need to do all the things in this song."

I KNOW PLACES

WRITERS Taylor Swift, Ryan Tedder

———

Amid the rampant tabloid scrutiny of her love life, Taylor found herself developing a new skill: hiding her relationships from prying eyes. She assures her love interest that they can escape the "hunters". The mounting production carries the feeling of being observed and then chased, particularly as we reach the crescendo of the pre-chorus' shouted "we run!". She is on alert, like prey, constantly wary of all the outsiders gunning for her. The imagery applies to fame, but finds a universal relatability in evoking a gossip-fuelled small town. The "shots" taken could be insults or paparazzi photos. The themes of secrecy and privacy become a priority in future albums, in particular *reputation, Lover* and *folklore*.

TOP On the red carpet at the Met Gala in 2014.

MIDDLE The 1989 World Tour reportedly took around ten months to plan and rehearse.

BOTTOM Taylor brings the big *1989* hits to The Eras Tour stage.

CLEAN

WRITERS Taylor Swift, Imogen Heap

Before the live performance of 'Clean' on each night of her 1989 World Tour, Taylor would give an inspirational speech over a meandering guitar solo. These addresses varied, but ultimately centred on key messages: even if you fall for a person (or a thing) that is bad for you, things will get better. The song itself is an emotional ballad about that clarifying moment when you realise you have overcome a heartbreak. The "flood" you faced might have been devastating, but you are renewed now. Although not her intended meaning, it has come to signify breaking from addiction or surviving dark times: a testament to her work's relatability.

WONDERLAND

WRITERS Taylor Swift, Max Martin, Shellback

Using fairytale iconography from *Alice in Wonderland*, Taylor tells the story of a whirlwind romance that drove both partners insane. In this synthy, fantastical production we hear about the warning signs, the outside pressure, and the downward spiral of the love that was destined to fail. Despite the madness, she is comforted by their shared good times – a thematic link to 'Wildest Dreams'. There are a number of rumours regarding the inspiration for the song, including one about her sexuality triggered by the use of the word "straight", which her team later dismissed.

> *'Clean' portrays the clarifying moment when you realise you have overcome heartbreak*

YOU ARE IN LOVE

WRITERS Taylor Swift, Jack Antonoff

The nostalgic, cinematic sound of 'You Are in Love' gives the feeling of it being a score to an 80s romance movie. It's inspired by the then relationship of Taylor's friends Jack Antonoff and Lena Dunham, and how they came to realise they had fallen for one another. The first verse is one partner realising in a small private moment together; in the second verse, we hear the moment the other partner realises they are too. Taylor describes it as… well, indescribable: it's seen, heard and felt even in the most quiet of moments. Witnessing love in this pure form makes Taylor realise why she has dedicated her life and career to capturing and articulating it.

1989 marked a turning point in Taylor's musical evolution.

NEW ROMANTICS

WRITERS Taylor Swift, Max Martin, Shellback

'New Romantics' is an anthemic testament to hopeless romantics. She is mocking her generation's (and her own) naïve, perhaps foolish, and ultimately more fun way of approaching relationships heart-first. Although outwardly critical of these "new romantics", she very much counts herself amongst them and considers them the "best" people. If you're going to have your heart broken, you may as well free fall, dancing, into it. It's a keenly self-aware assessment from Taylor, who had endured years of criticism for the pace and intensity of her relationships. The song became a fan favourite, and it soundtracked the official promotional video of the 1989 World Tour.

NOW THAT WE DON'T TALK

WRITERS Taylor Swift, Jack Antonoff

This song glitters from the contempt Taylor holds for its main character. It acts almost like a lecture given to an ex who initially cut her off, but now is perhaps expecting her to still play the role of therapist or friend. Taylor has to remind herself of all the negatives of the relationship (relatably, by calling her mother) and that she no longer has to pretend to be someone she isn't. We know from elsewhere in the catalogue that this lover missed multiple opportunities ('Say Don't Go') and "faded" away (unreciprocated love being a core theme of *Red*), so her dismissal feels all the more justified. It's witty, deriding, and deeply catchy.

> *'Sweeter than Fiction' marked the start of a prolific partnership with Jack Antonoff*

'SLUT!'

WRITERS Taylor Swift, Jack Antonoff, Patrik Berger

The dreamier, more resigned sister song to 'Blank Space'. Taylor is willing to put up with being unfairly slut-shamed by the media if it means she gets to keep her true love. She described *1989* as being "New York", whereas 'Slut!' felt much more "California", hence its exclusion from the original 2014 release ("Sometimes, thematically, I just had these little weird rules in my head", she explained on Tumblr Music). Rife with wordplay, it features Taylor's trademark reimagining of common phrases – like being lovesick over her bed. She accepts that she alone will "pay the price" for their relationship, yet his role as a gentleman means she does not blame him for this inequality.

SUBURBAN LEGENDS

WRITERS Taylor Swift, Jack Antonoff

When Taylor ponders on her legacy, it's often in the context of her hometown. We see this in the trophies held up for her town from 'Long Live', and astonished friends from home in 'You're on Your Own Kid'. 'Suburban Legends' takes this image to its full potential: here is a couple whose love story will become notorious. It portrays a familiar backdrop of an unequal relationship: this time in the "currency" of coolness, and of outsiders' perceptions damaging their romantic chances. It's unclear whether the relationship ends because of their inequality, or because of this pressure – Taylor once again has to break her own heart to save her partner the trouble.

SAY DON'T GO

WRITERS Taylor Swift, Diane Warren

The rock-tinged production is the musical sibling of the pining 'I Wish You Would' and 'All You Had to Do Was Stay', where the simplicity of Taylor's advice is mirrored. It tells the story of a relationship that she reluctantly ends, and the silence that followed. Taylor feels that her love is unreciprocated, even in its final moments. The production kicks up a notch at the turning point in the narrative (a favourite technique of hers), when we shift from soft and gently pleading to a far more accusatory and frustrated tone. This was her first collaboration with songwriting legend Diane Warren, but maybe it won't be the last. Discussing the possibility of working with Taylor again, Warren told *Rolling Stone*: "If she's down, I'd be down. That would be awesome."

SWEETER THAN FICTION

WRITERS Taylor Swift, Jack Antonoff

Appearing on the soundtrack to the film *One Chance*, 'Sweeter than Fiction' was never meant to happen. Taylor's record label at the time discouraged her from releasing the song due to fears of overexposure – but having seen the film, she was undeterred and teamed up with Jack Antonoff to write and produce the song. That pivotal collaboration was the first time the pair had worked together, marking the start of a prolific partnership. The result was this 80s-style pop song with self-empowerment-themed lyrics that are sugary without being saccharine. Released a year before *1989*, it was nominated at the Golden Globes for Best Original Song, and hinted at Taylor taking a further step away from country into pure pop.

Spotlight on...

IS IT OVER NOW?

WRITERS

Taylor Swift, Jack Antonoff

Fans consider 'Is It Over Now?' as the sequel to 'Out of the Woods': there are the same rhetorical repeated questions, the same anxiety and the same attention to detail. Where it differs, dramatically, is in the emotion. Rather than the hopeful panic of trying to get through hardship, 'Is It Over Now?' is resentful and frustrated as Taylor tries to define when exactly this relationship has ended.

It is searing, deriding and unflinchingly critical. Littered with scandalous details of infidelity, arguments and attention-seeking, the song offers a new level of insight into the relationship. It's largely believed to be chronicling her relationship with Harry Styles, due to the references to a snowmobile accident they are said to have been in. The song sees Taylor taking responsibility for her role in their demise, but she's no less scathing towards him as a result.

When releasing the track in 2023, Taylor noted its thematic similarities to both 'I Wish You Would' and 'Out of the Woods', which is why the song was cut from the original 2014 release. She must have been glad to reverse that decision for *1989 (Taylor's Version)*, as it went on to become her lucky 13th No.1 single.

Taylor's Version
COMING
SOON...

REPUTATION

4 WEEKS AT
NO.1*

Taylor rose from the ashes of 2016's scandals with this darker yet surprisingly romantic album, declaring "there will be no explanation, just reputation"

WORDS BY FARRAH FROST

Album Artwork: Big Machine Records. Images: Getty Images.
*Source: *Billboard* 200, correct as of 2 May 2024.

LEFT The Reputation Stadium Tour set design included plenty of snake references.
RIGHT Taylor created this album as her "defence mechanism" after years of media scrutiny.

...READY FOR IT?

WRITERS Taylor Swift, Max Martin, Shellback, Ali Payami

—

When the thundering baseline opens the album, listeners are confronted: this is not the Taylor Swift you thought you knew. The song purportedly is about finding your "partner in crime" to face the world with, introducing the album's core themes of reputation, secrecy, and falling in love despite the world. However, the track serves a greater purpose for Taylor's musical presence as a whole. It is a declaration that she has overcome, and she's bringing her best work with her in the loot bag: the stakes are higher, the romance is edgier, the imagery is sharper, the wordplay is fiercer. We're invited along for the ride, ready or not.

END GAME
(FEAT. ED SHEERAN AND FUTURE)

WRITERS Taylor Swift, Max Martin, Shellback, Ed Sheeran, Nayvadius Wilburn

—

Hanging on the metaphor of becoming someone's happily ever after, the song shares perspectives with celebrated lyricists Future and Ed Sheeran. The three pitch themselves to their respective loves: bad reputations included. The "big enemies" are a clear acknowledgement of the public feuds Taylor was emerging from at the time. It is a line of Ed's verse that seems most pertinent: he admits that all aspects of the relationship will "end up" in his music: a marker of this album's autobiographical nature and a forewarning of Taylor's future albums – notably *Midnights,* which is in part inspired by the same relationship as *reputation* from the perspective of five years later.

I DID SOMETHING BAD

WRITERS Taylor Swift, Max Martin, Shellback

—

One of three *reputation* tracks addressing Taylor's public downfall in 2016 (along with 'Look What You Made Me Do' and 'This Is Why We Can't Have Nice Things'). We have familiar Swiftian territory: the colour red, flying and travel, the burning fire… However, rather than the typical innocence she conveys, Taylor admits her crimes and revels in them despite the witch hunt. Comparisons can be made to the songs satirising perceptions of her love life ('Blank Space') and mocking rumours about her ('Who's Afraid of Little Old Me?'); similarly here, Taylor is reclaiming the idea she is the villain with dramatic effect.

DON'T BLAME ME

WRITERS Taylor Swift, Max Martin, Shellback

—

Abundant with religious imagery and gospel elements, 'Don't Blame Me' asks for sacred forgiveness for her sins given her circumstances: she is addicted to her lover. Previous albums only made subtle drug references (if any), indicating that a more mature suite of themes was open to Taylor going forward. The addiction is so overwhelming that she will allow her paramour to decide her name, instigate a fall from grace, or even go insane. The song makes one of several references to *The Great Gatsby* on the album, when she is turned from poison ivy to "your daisy", the name of F Scott Fitzgerald's heroine. The drug, illicit love and religious references on 'Don't Blame Me' have drawn comparison to the sonically and thematically similar 'Take Me to Church' by Hozier.

Spotlight on...
DELICATE

WRITERS Taylor Swift, Max Martin, Shellback

This is *reputation*'s first admission of vulnerability. Where the previous tracks satirise, disregard or almost enjoy the challenge presented to her by her tarnished reputation, 'Delicate' is a more confessional, nervous song. Over vocoded vocals and synth beats, Taylor asks her lover for reassurance that everything is okay: almost giving him the room he needs to leave if the mounting pressure is too much.

Secrecy and fame references abound, yet the song feels universal. 'Delicate' represents the very early stages of a relationship, when you aren't yet sure where you stand, you try to maintain an air of "cool", and you open yourself up to hurt. The music video is abundant with her trademark Easter eggs and Swiftian imagery from *The Great Gatsby*-inspired outfits, dancing in the pouring rain (à la 'Fearless'), and a number of literal signs featuring lyrics, names and a dive bar rumoured to be the birthplace of her relationship with Alywn.

Mirroring the song's slow build, it was something of a sleeper hit. Despite generating high praise from critics and fans as some of her best work, the song had a slow-burn effect on the charts, and eventually became the album's most successful radio hit.

Spotlight on...

LOOK WHAT YOU MADE ME DO

SEE PAGE 69.

SO IT GOES...

WRITERS Taylor Swift, Max Martin, Shellback, Oscar Görres

—

Sexual themes had only been fleetingly mentioned in Taylor's prior work – the most explicit probably being "say it with your hands" lyric from *Red*'s 'Treacherous'. This song shows us a fully embraced sexual persona for Taylor, where the throes of passion are vivid. It maintains the album's core theme of secrecy: her lover is an illusionist, they must meet in darkness. When Taylor asks who between them is counting, we hear her playfully count in the next beat. This is referenced under less amorous circumstances years later in 'High Infidelity'.

GORGEOUS

WRITERS Taylor Swift, Max Martin, Shellback

—

Despite a similar sound to the rest of *reputation*, 'Gorgeous' is a much more classic pop love song. It's a frisky tribute to infatuation, Taylor style. Inspired by Joe Alwyn's beauty and its effect on her, she's playful, shy and daring all at once. The older boyfriend mentioned in the song seems a clear reference to her ex Calvin Harris, and further propels speculation over the timing of her relationships. The song opens with an adorable child's voice – Taylor revealed this was James Reynolds, the daughter of her friends Blake Lively and Ryan Reynolds.

GETAWAY CAR

WRITERS Taylor Swift, Jack Antonoff

—

This song fuels further speculation on the timing and motivations of Taylor's relationships. Revisiting the language of '...Ready for It?' with love as a criminal enterprise, it implies infidelity with "traitors", and highlights the media scrutiny she faces. Largely understood as a metaphor for a relationship that helped her escape another, the song has become a fan favourite for its fizzing production, excellently executed concept and one of her strongest bridges. In a memorable clip shared as part of the *Making of a Song* YouTube series, Taylor and Jack Antonoff are seen finessing the bridge – a moment with palpable excitement as the duo reach an extraordinary creative flow together.

TOP Taylor's *reputation* outfit for Eras features bejewelled snakes.
MIDDLE Performing 'Dress' during the Reputation Stadium Tour.
BOTTOM During the 2018 tour, Taylor sang a medley of 'Long Live' and 'New Year's Day' at the piano.

KING OF MY HEART

WRITERS Taylor Swift, Max Martin, Shellback

Taylor described this as narrating distinct phases of a relationship within each section of the song, serving as a timeline of her previous few years and the gear changes in her life. Beginning the track by resigning herself to a life of solitude, the electro kicks in when Taylor meets the object of her affection. Priorities change from isolation as a form of self-inflicted punishment, to privacy as a form of protection. She experiences true luxury: your lover's lips. Taylor has often upended ideas of luxury – rather than materialistic, her preferred opulence is peace (as in 'the lakes', 'Paper Rings', 'Paris' and 'I Hate It Here' in later albums).

THIS IS WHY WE CAN'T HAVE NICE THINGS

WRITERS Taylor Swift, Jack Antonoff

A comedic, gleeful song. Taylor admonishes the villains in her life as though they are impatient toddlers. She threw big parties, invited people on stage, was lavish as a friend: they sold her out. (This was likely her "golden era" of *1989* success.) She was forgiving and graceful: they made vulgar art about her, then lied about it. The second verse is widely accepted to be about her feud with Kanye West and Kim Kardashian – the phone call references a key dispute in their rocky relationship. In the end, she raises a glass to her real friends, lover and family – and has a good laugh about it all.

> *Taylor demonstrates her capacity to layer meaning across her whole catalogue*

DANCING WITH OUR HANDS TIED

WRITERS Taylor Swift, Max Martin, Shellback, Oscar Holter

The banjos of Taylor's early albums are a distant memory: this is a house-infused dance track with synths and heavy bass drops. The new soundscape is, however, accompanied with familiar Swift lyrics. It is an exploration of her recurring fear that the outside world will ultimately end her relationships, something we see throughout her discography ('Wonderland', 'Anti-Hero', 'The Lucky One' and 'peace' for example). It is also an early recolouring of love from being red to "golden" – something she explores in greater depth in 'Daylight'. Although the song is ostensibly about fame, Taylor retains relatability as ever; the pressures in question could just as easily be cultural or social media-fuelled.

CALL IT WHAT YOU WANT

WRITERS Taylor Swift, Jack Antonoff

In isolation, this is a charming love song about being at peace. In the context of Taylor's entire discography, it's a layered masterpiece. Fans drew a comparison between the bridge's rescuing and running away imagery with the 'Love Story' chorus (even before the song was released: lyrics were teased on social media). She also nods to 'Castles Crumbling' and "burning" love as in 'Begin Again'. A particularly strong narrative connection is to 'Blank Space': the "daydream" and "storms". This is an intentional reminder of the exaggerated love-defying, boy-mad Taylor satirised in that *1989* hit. By burying these links to her other work, Taylor demonstrates her capacity to layer meaning across her whole catalogue.

DRESS

WRITERS Taylor Swift, Jack Antonoff

Dresses have been a favourite image of Taylor's throughout her albums. They're mentioned across her catalogue: 'Tim McGraw', 'The Moment I Knew' and 'Wildest Dreams' for example. They represent a variety of things: joy, innocence, status. 'Dress' adds a new meaning to the list: lust. This song's outfit has been bought purely to be discarded on the bedroom floor. Her lover sees her in her naked truth: including the witch hunt scars and mistakes. Given the haircuts described, fans conclude this song is about Alwyn – and it also reveals a little of her relationship with Tom Hiddleston ("my rebounds"), perhaps another reason for the album's central theme of privacy and secrecy.

NEW YEAR'S DAY

WRITERS Taylor Swift, Jack Antonoff

'New Year's Day' is set apart from the rest of the album: sonically, it is the only acoustic track and lyrically it is a return to Taylor's much softer side. She has written many songs cementing true love as one that thrives in mundanity (such as 'Paper Rings' and 'Ours'). While Taylor wants the parties, big nights and bright lights, she also wants the unremarkable days that follow. Wanting his "midnights" is later referenced by the concept of her tenth album of the same name. In a way, the promise written on "the last page" is as much a reassurance to her fanbase as it is to her lover: the old Taylor's romantic country roots aren't dead after all.

Spotlight on...

LOOK WHAT YOU MADE ME DO

WRITERS Taylor Swift, Jack Antonoff, Fred Fairbrass, Richard Fairbrass, Rob Manzoli

Not one to shy away from melodrama, Taylor exploded back into public life with 'Look What You Made Me Do'. Taking the bull by the horns, she addresses the main scandals that drove her into isolation in 2016 head-on. Accompanied by an Easter egg-stuffed music video extravaganza, this song sent fans and critics alike into speculation overdrive. A lyrical and visual feast: Taylor is no stranger to satirising her public image ('Blank Space'), and claps back at many of the insults she faced: money-grabber, duplicitous ghostwriter, fame-hungry, serial dater and – most pertinently – the snake. This is the dawn of the snake: the emblem Taylor reclaims.

The glitzy and bombastic production was a shockwave to the general public who associated Taylor with cheery pop or heartbroken ballads. The interpolation of Right Said Fred's 'I'm Too Sexy' and the electro-pop production hinted at the darker, sultry soundscape of the *reputation*. Combined with enough Easter eggs to overwhelm even the most eager Swiftie, it seems Taylor was telling us that if we were going to talk, she was going to give us something to talk about. Boosted by this frenzy, it broke streaming records, placed atop the charts and garnered multiple award nominations. The old Taylor is dead, long live the new Taylor.

reputation
Taylor's Version

COMING SOON...

Performing '…Ready for It?' on The Eras Tour in Sydney, Australia.

LOVER

1 WEEK AT
NO. 1*

Taylor's first self-owned album blends cheerful pop and searing
introspection, exploring love in all its guises

WORDS BY FARRAH FROST

I FORGOT THAT YOU EXISTED

WRITERS Taylor Swift, Louis Bell, Adam King Feeney

—

The opener to her first self-owned album sets the carefree tone of a new era for Taylor. 'I Forgot That You Existed' chronicles the moment she realises that she is happy enough in her new life to hold no love or hate, "just indifference" to the way things were. It is rumoured to be about her 15-month relationship with DJ Calvin Harris, but equally applies to any 'hater' in her life. Perhaps of all her songwriting, the clear premise of this track delivers her most impactful insult: you were simply not worth writing a song about.

Spotlight on...

CRUEL SUMMER

SEE PAGE 75.

LOVER

WRITERS Taylor Swift (and Shawn Mendes, Scott Harris on the remix)

—

Fans and critics alike consider this song one of the greatest examples of Taylor's songwriting. She is said to have set out to create a timeless song that could be a first dance at a wedding – whether 50 years ago or today – so she only used instruments that would have been available back in the 1970s, lending the track a dreamy, retro vibe. The lyrics denote a simple, beautiful relationship: the bare honesty of the love is found in simple mundanity, their acts of quiet kindness, and in the existential questions repeated throughout. The bridge reads like wedding vows; this is Taylor at her most romantic. A surprise remix with Shawn Mendes was later released, transforming the song into a delightful duet.

THE MAN

WRITERS Taylor Swift, Joel Little

—

'The Man' is really Taylor's first overtly political statement in her music, although certainly not her last. It explores the contradictory nature of patriarchy through a simple premise: "If I were a man, I'd be THE man". Her successes and relationships are scrutinised, ridiculed and overlooked for the simple fact that she's a woman. The song is a rallying cry for women frustrated by a male-dominated world. It is much poppier and maybe less 'mature' than future tracks that criticise the patriarchy, notably 'mad woman', instead positioned as Taylor expressing frustration perhaps among friends, or hyping herself up alone.

TOP Playing 'Lover' during the 2019 American Music Awards.
MIDDLE A portrait from the 2019 AMAs red carpet.
BOTTOM Performing 'The Man' during The Eras Tour.

Album Artwork: Republic Records. Images: Getty Images & Alamy. *Source Billboard 200, correct as of 2 May 2024.

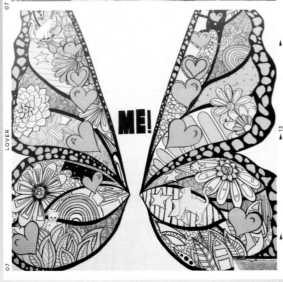

THE ARCHER

WRITERS Taylor Swift, Jack Antonoff

—

Possibly a reference to her star sign (Sagittarius' symbol is an archer), this track is a mature and introspective look at a relationship. The song perfectly encapsulates feelings of anxiety: the slow-burning production builds as the worries and fears grow; the lyrics detail her baseless fears and the sickening feeling that her lover will see her and all her faults. This song is a self-reflection on Taylor's habit of seeing the worst in herself, and on the assumed impossibility of loving her. It is vulnerable and haunting, following Taylor's 'track five' tradition of placing a deeply emotional song as the fifth entry on each album.

I THINK HE KNOWS

WRITERS Taylor Swift, Jack Antonoff

—

This pulsing and bright pop song is a cheeky and playful tribute to all the things unsaid in a happy relationship. It's a track tinged with the delight of inside jokes and quiet confidence. A fun Easter egg appears in the lyrics: the 16th Avenue she skips down is a reference to Music Row, a road in Nashville where she reportedly wrote many songs. It also flips a common Swiftian image of being driven ('Our Song', 'Getaway Car', 'Style') when she informs her lover "I'll drive" as they follow the "sparks" together, signifying a fresh confidence from Taylor.

 Song bridges are something of a speciality for Taylor, and 'Cruel Summer' has one of her finest

MISS AMERICANA & THE HEARTBREAK PRINCE

WRITERS Taylor Swift, Joel Little

—

This high school-themed song is a political statement. The 2020 documentary *Miss Americana*, filmed between the Reputation Stadium Tour and *Lover*'s release, follows Taylor's developing confidence in expressing her political opinions publicly. The namesake song uses some of Taylor's favourite imagery – that of high schools – as a loose metaphor for her disillusionment with US politics. Although the song can also be interpreted as a love story of a young couple vowing to escape their small town together, it has widely been viewed as Taylor's clearest musical disappointments in America's political landscape, noting her own pageantry role as 'Miss Americana' and glories fading before her eyes.

Spotlight on...
CRUEL SUMMER

WRITERS Taylor Swift, Jack Antonoff, Annie Clark

A pop song masterclass and a quintessential Swift song. The synth-pop track houses perhaps her catchiest melody and recaps a summer longing for a romance that lies tantalisingly out of reach. The lyrics tell a story of a frustrated narrator feeling unmoored in a new relationship and risking her pride for the potential lover. It features many of Taylor's favourite references – emotions as colours, secrets and hiding, vulnerability and anxiety in love – and her trademark wordplay.

Song bridges are something of a speciality for Taylor, and the pulsing, drunken admission of her love in 'Cruel Summer' has been reviewed as one of her finest. Enjoyed by fans and critics alike, the track ranked in *Rolling Stone*'s 'Greatest Songs of All Time' list.

The track was originally slated for a single roll-out in 2020, but these plans were scuppered by the global pandemic. However, it gained momentum four years after *Lover*'s release as it dominated the opening set of The Eras Tour, and was eventually released on 13 June 2023. This sleeper hit secured Taylor's tenth No.1 single and broke a number of charting records – some of which she had previously held herself. As of 8 May 2024, 'Cruel Summer' is set to surpass 'Anti-Hero' as the longest-charting *Billboard* single of her career so far, with 52 weeks and counting on the Hot 100.

Performing at the iHeartRadio Wango Tango event in June 2019.

PAPER RINGS

WRITERS Taylor Swift, Jack Antonoff

—

Who needs shiny things?! 'Paper Rings' is a thumping, chipper song that exclaims Taylor will forgo any luxuries for the ultimate prized object: her love. It features familiar Swiftie tropes: romanticising mundanity (such as in 'Ours', 'Mine', 'London Boy'), references to wine as indicators of the status of the relationship (as in 'Dress', 'Maroon'), money and specifically eschewing its relevance in relationships (as in 'New Romantics', 'King of My Heart'). It also includes a quick countdown, which in true Taylor style adds up to her lucky number 13. 'Paper Rings' achieves what many pop songs aim for: to be good honest fun.

LONDON BOY

WRITERS Taylor Swift, Jack Antonoff, Cautious Clay, Mark Anthony Spears

—

Two cities recur throughout Taylor's catalogue: New York and London. While New York represents something of a home to her, London has often represented a beloved yet distant destination. 'London Boy' hones in on this narrative, turning this proud American into a certified Anglophile. We tour the capital alongside her as she details the ways in which she loves being shown around – and shown off in – her lover's hometown (Londoners were tickled by the geographic improbability of the tour she describes). The track also opens with a curious vox pop of Idris Elba discussing his favourite London hobby.

> " *New York is a meaningful city to Taylor, representing freedom, opportunity, and being one's true self* "

CORNELIA STREET

WRITERS Taylor Swift

—

The real Cornelia Street, in New York, is where Taylor lived while renovating her other apartment in the city. Grounded in this reality, the song explores the depths of her love and the impact losing it would have. It's a romantic song, yet exemplifies a lover's anxiety (as she does in the more forlorn 'The Archer'). New York is a meaningful city to Taylor, representing freedom, opportunity, and being one's true self. To lose this love equates to losing all of this. At the Paris 2019 City of Lovers concert, she informed fans that the song was her "most personal", and as if to prove just how personal, she revealed that she wrote it in the bathtub.

SOON YOU'LL GET BETTER (FEAT. THE CHICKS)

WRITERS Taylor Swift, Jack Antonoff

—

Lifelong heroes of Taylor's, and her mother's favourite band, The Chicks can be heard harmonising alongside Taylor in this gentle, emotional ballad. The song is beseeching and quiet – Taylor convincing herself and her mother that she will soon recover from her illness. Andrea Swift, her mum, was first diagnosed with cancer in 2015, and again in 2018. Taylor previously stated she'd never perform the song, and reportedly left the Secret Sessions fan listening party when the track played. However, she did make an exception for the charity *One World: Together at Home* coronavirus response event.

DEATH BY A THOUSAND CUTS

WRITERS Taylor Swift, Jack Antonoff

—

Ancient torture methods are a strange metaphor for a breakup, but not for Taylor. The song charts the despondency and variety of ways that heartbreak hurts. It features an emphatic bridge and some of her strongest lyrics – notably including asking traffic lights for advice. Her search isn't limited to inanimate objects – she looks through the "boarded" windows of love and across her body to find any part of her untouched by pain. At the *Tiny Desk* live performance, she explained that as someone known for her break-up songs, she was worried that while she was in a happy relationship, her skills would be lost forever. 'Death by a Thousand Cuts' proves otherwise.

FALSE GOD

WRITERS Taylor Swift, Jack Antonoff

—

'False God' is a more nocturnal sound from Taylor. The sensual saxophone-led track accompanies breathy, meandering vocals and charged lyrics. The song charts the push and pull of a couple who are so devoted to their "sacred" relationship that they may just make it after all, in part due to their sexual compatibility. The sultry sound is a revelation for Taylor, allowing her to indulge in more mature themes. The use of religious imagery isn't new territory for her – past tracks 'Holy Ground' and 'Our Song' invoked holiness for various effects – and she continues to employ this symbolism in her later work, notably on 'Would've, Could've, Should've' and 'Guilty as Sin?'.

YOU NEED TO CALM DOWN

WRITERS Taylor Swift, Joel Little

Taylor is no stranger to "haters". Until this song, her foremost acknowledgement of them was her mega-hit 'Shake It Off'. 'You Need to Calm Down' revisits her dissidents with aplomb and a music video bursting with pop culture references.

The track skewers these haters with a line they so often direct towards their victims: "you need to calm down." A verse is dedicated to pitting women against each other (the music video resolves a feud between Taylor and Katy Perry), and we have a brief mention of the "snakes" that infamously tried to dethrone her.

It is also her most explicitly supportive song for the LGBTQ+ community. The music video featured multiple queer pop culture icons including the cast of Netflix's *Queer Eye* and stars from *RuPaul's Drag Race*. Some critics expressed concern that it downplays the insidious nature of hate by demoting these people to simple internet trolls and the like. Nevertheless, Taylor was awarded the GLAAD Vanguard Award in recognition of her public allyship to the LGBTQ+ community in 2020, in part due to their shout-out in the song.

LEFT Performing 'ME!' with Brendon Urie at the 2019 *Billboard* Music Awards.
RIGHT With her backing singers: Jeslyn Gorman, Eliotte Nicole, Melanie Nyema and Kamilah Marshall.

AFTERGLOW

WRITERS Taylor Swift, Louis Bell, Adam King Feeney

Possibly the narrative follow-up to 'The Archer', 'Afterglow' is an apology to her lover for sabotaging their relationship. The "combat" she is poised for in 'The Archer' has seemingly come to fruition. Apologies are a common theme for Taylor – as in 'Back to December' and 'betty'. Taking place after a big fight, she pleads with her partner for reassurance and forgiveness. The song features "burning" imagery: the idea that a relationship is something susceptible to flames also comes up in 'ivy' and 'hoax'; while fire also appears to burn reputations, as in 'Don't Blame Me' and 'my tears ricochet'. Here, Taylor hopes to rekindle her love from the glowing embers and ashes of the relationship.

ME! (FEAT. BRENDON URIE)

WRITERS Taylor Swift, Joel Little, Brendon Urie

Bouncy and impossibly catchy, *Lover*'s lead single pounced into the charts. It's an upbeat, outrageously cheerful bop, championing individuality and confidence – possibly influenced by a glut of self-empowerment songs when the album was being written ('This Is Me', from *The Greatest Showman* soundtrack was a runaway hit in 2018). It was Taylor's first lead single featuring a collaborator; she had always wanted to work with Panic! at the Disco's Brendon Urie, but was waiting for the right song: "When I wrote this chorus I KNEW," she explained. It was a marked tonal change from the darker production of her previous album *reputation*, a testament to Taylor's versatility.

IT'S NICE TO HAVE A FRIEND

WRITERS Taylor Swift, Louis Bell, Adam King Feeney

The uncomplicated story of childhood sweethearts. The song stretches Taylor's storytelling ability: the entire thing is delivered in three-to-five syllabic vignettes and totals in at just 2 minutes 30 seconds, making it her shortest track at the time. Deceptively complex, the song is a masterclass in brevity. It has fascinated reviewers, who have noted the departure in style and form (No chorus! No bridge!) from the rest of her catalogue. The ghostly choir backdrop and plinking harp are only interrupted by church bells and trumpeting, almost giving the song an eerie feel. Despite the atypical Swift sound and structure, we can recognise her favourite imagery – schoolyards and weddings are a familiar backdrop for Taylor.

DAYLIGHT

WRITERS Taylor Swift

The sense that Taylor is "emerging" into something new appears in many Swift songs ('Out of the Woods', 'Clean', 'Afterglow'). This rebirth gives her new opportunity, and in the case of 'Daylight' it recolours love from "burning" red to golden. This colour switch lyric has been widely regarded as her growth from the visceral, wild love described in 'Red' into a calmer, more soothing shade. The song closes the album out with a spoken word epilogue from Taylor, explaining that she wants to move on from being defined by the negativity in her life – a clear nod to *reputation*'s central theme, and instead wants to be defined by the positives.

FOLKLORE

8 WEEKS AT NO. 1*

Amid the pandemic, *folklore* came as a complete surprise with a radically new sound,
mostly fictional narratives, and no rollout to promote the album

WORDS BY FARRAH FROST

THE 1

WRITERS Taylor Swift, Aaron Dessner

—

The opening line – one of her finest – reintroduces us to Taylor. In just eight words, she lets us know that she has moved on from the more bombastic and brightly lit era of her life. The song is a grown-up reflection on a relationship that didn't work out, despite their good times. Rather than being regretful, it is warm and witty as she wonders where they went wrong and whether great loves can ever really last. The song characterises Taylor as the driving force behind the relationship's downfall – the narrative counterpart to 'The Archer' or 'Afterglow'.

CARDIGAN

WRITERS Taylor Swift, Aaron Dessner

—

This is one of the three songs featured in *folklore*'s Teenage Love Triangle alongside 'betty' and 'august'. In 'cardigan' we hear the perspective of Betty, the girl who loses her lover to another. Wise beyond her years, Betty delivers a warm and detailed reasoning for her decision to accept him back: despite causing her scars, he will be the one to draw stars around them. Containing some of Taylor's most celebrated lyrics, she invokes familiar fairytale imagery with Peter Pan references and rhyming couplets throughout. This is also the song that launched an iconic sell-out Swift merch: the cardigan.

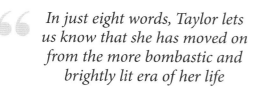

> *In just eight words, Taylor lets us know that she has moved on from the more bombastic and brightly lit era of her life*

THE LAST GREAT AMERICAN DYNASTY

WRITERS Taylor Swift, Aaron Dessner

—

A clear nod to her country songwriting roots, Taylor here tells us the story of the real-life Rebecca Harkness: the Golden Age muse whose eccentricity and exuberant high society lifestyle cast her as an outsider in her coastal Rhode Island village. It's a testament to Taylor's world-building capabilities that in just a few phrases we can perfectly envision the garish wedding, scandalised neighbours and sumptuous lifestyle. Taylor finds commonality with Rebecca – women with tarnished reputations who live their best life regardless. The song also features a classic Swiftian plot twist: it unfolds that the mansion at the centre of the story is now Taylor's home.

Album Artwork: Republic Records. Images: Getty Images. *Source *Billboard* 200, correct as of 2 May 2024.

TOP With *folklore* collaborators Aaron Dessner and Jack Antonoff.
MIDDLE Taylor on the red carpet at the 2020 Golden Globes.
BOTTOM An Eras performance of 'the last great american dynasty'.

TOP The magic of *folklore* was brought to life during The Eras Tour.
MIDDLE Pandemic chic at the Grammys in 2021.
BOTTOM Taylor embraced a cottagecore aesthetic on this album.

EXILE (FEAT. BON IVER)

WRITERS Taylor Swift, William Bowery, Justin Vernon

—

This affecting ballad with Bon Iver delivers the story of broken hearts and miscommunications. The first verse is his perspective, the second hers, and the remainder is their dialogue, singing over one another, never truly hearing what the other is saying. The call and response delivers the contradictions that led to the end of the relationship in a rising cacophony of excuses. It's a rare joint perspective for Taylor, who usually resorts to imagination to give the other half of the story. 'Exile' became Bon Iver's first Top Ten chart hit and Taylor's 28th. The song was one of several co-written with the mysterious William Bowery, later revealed to be a pseudonym of her then partner Joe Alywn.

Spotlight on...

MY TEARS RICOCHET

SEE PAGE 84.

MIRRORBALL

WRITERS Taylor Swift, Jack Antonoff

—

This song is a sensitive moment of self-reflection as Taylor talks of her ability to reflect whatever you want to see in her back to you – a mirror in a million pieces. The need for external validation is powerful, something she will do anything for. In context of the 2020 pandemic lockdowns, there is a sense of panic as her opportunities to shine are gone, performing to an empty room. Though the song is a metaphor for fame, there is Taylor's classic universal relatability: its message resonates with anyone who has felt themselves desperate to be seen.

SEVEN

WRITERS Taylor Swift, Aaron Dessner

—

The nostalgic 'seven' invokes a childhood friendship. A story of innocence, unselfconsciousness and enduring friendships, yet there is a dark undertone. The listener picks up on signs that the friend at the heart of the song is experiencing some kind of suffering. The secrets sworn, the father's bad mood, the plots to run away. It is reminiscent of the track 'It's Nice to Have a Friend' on *Lover*, which also revisits youthful innocence. In the *Long Pond Studio Sessions* documentary, Taylor states the song contains the most important lyric on the album: "Just like a folk song, our love will be passed on."

Taylor performed a medley of *folklore* and *evermore* songs at the Grammys in 2021.

Spotlight on...
MY TEARS RICOCHET

WRITERS Taylor Swift

———

Taylor here notes how her hurt rebounds and impacts those around her, and how galling it is that the villain here is impervious to the pain they caused her. Fans believe the inspiration for the song is the anger she felt towards Scott Borchetta, her former manager. Borchetta became a central character in her infamous masters dispute. The "betrayal" at the centre of their fallout is that Borchetta sold her masters to someone Taylor has long felt bullied and ridiculed by: Scooter Braun. She questions his guilt – he hears her stolen songs as he tries to sleep, and he stands dolefully at her wake wearing the riches she made for him.

A master of subtle nods to her own work, each line of the first chorus twists lyrics from five songs off the albums she created alongside Borchetta: the grace in 'State of Grace', heroes flying in 'Superman', dying 'Look What You Made Me Do', name cursing 'That's the Way I Loved You', staying 'All You Had to Do Was Stay', and most explicitly the tears dropping and now ricocheting from her guitar as in *Taylor Swift* debut. A self-referential masterclass.

AUGUST

WRITERS Taylor Swift, Jack Antonoff

The second song in the Teenage Love Triangle trilogy, in 'august' Taylor details the summer fling as the "other woman" (she is named Augusta or Augustine according to Taylor). The protaganist reminisces on the love she almost had, even if she knew deep down it was never going to last. The wondrous, dreamy soundscape of the track has a nostalgic, yearning feel and hopeful lyrics. Innocence – and the loss of it – is a theme Taylor revisits again and again in her work (such as in 'Would've Could've Should've' and 'Perfectly Good Heart') – and 'august' certainly has a feel of a naïve protagonist being inevitably hurt.

INVISIBLE STRING

WRITERS Taylor Swift, Aaron Dessner

Fate and a love's inevitability set the romantic backdrop of the happenstances and coincidences charting Taylor and her lover's separate lives that would eventually lead them to one another. Destiny is similarly explored in 'Timeless', but in 'invisible string' the imaginative thread is led by their real lives, not alternate realities. The premise is tied to the ancient Chinese spiritual theory that our fate is stitched together like threads. Spiritual motifs recur in Taylor's work, with holy references in 'False God', 'Don't Blame Me' and 'Guilty as Sin?', for example. This is a charming and intimate song.

> " *Innocence – and the loss of it – is a theme Taylor revisits again and again in her work*

THIS IS ME TRYING

WRITERS Taylor Swift, Jack Antonoff

Telling another fictional story, here Taylor tries to convey to the listener that even though what they see might not be exceptional, or even good enough, the protagonist is trying. There are implications of alcoholism and even suicidal ideation. It's about putting your best effort in and ultimately coming up short – something any listener can relate to. The haunting echo of the song's title in the chorus is an unnerving note of desperation: we see the once-lauded protagonist hit rock bottom. This idea of becoming rejected is also present in 'Nothing New'. It's these themes that fans often attribute to the song being considered one of her most heartbreaking.

MAD WOMAN

WRITERS Taylor Swift, Aaron Dessner

While *Lover*'s 'The Man' is an upbeat girl-power hype song, 'mad woman' is the older, more measured and furious ballad. Most directly inspired by her song ownership rights feud, but with possible connections to the public breakdown of her civility with Kanye West, the lyrics detail the experience of being wronged as a woman. From the disbelief that she would dare to react, the gaslighting and downplaying, to being labelled as "crazy". Taylor spares no scorn, with a scandalous callout of the bad guy's alleged infidelity (rumoured to be Scooter Braun, but possibly Kanye West), and a rare but emphatically delivered profanity.

ILLICIT AFFAIRS

WRITERS Taylor Swift, Jack Antonoff

Infidelity, from all its angles, is a familiar story for Taylor's songs, for example 'Getaway Car' and 'Should've Said No'. In 'illicit affairs', we see the affair in devastating retrospect: the ghost of a real relationship that could've been something beautiful but was ultimately doomed from the start. The protagonist is arguing with her ex about how he has mistreated her, despite all the hoops she had to jump through. It's a relationship that never meant as much to him as it did her. Delivering one of her most emphatic and emotionally charged bridges, Taylor allows herself to be bowled over by the anger she has buried in previous verses.

EPIPHANY

WRITERS Taylor Swift, Aaron Dessner

It's this song that cements *folklore* as a pandemic album. Completely written and produced at the height of the Covid-19 global shutdown, 'epiphany' draws a comparison between wartime and the coronavirus response. She compares the unspeakable things a soldier witnesses with the traumatising experiences of Covid medics. The protagonists yearn for some sort of revelation to help them process the horrors they have seen. Battle imagery in the Swiftian world typically refers to the pursuit of love through internal or external pressures, but Taylor draws this powerful comparison to intentionally spotlight the selfless work of the global medical community.

Spotlight on...
BETTY

WRITERS Taylor Swift, William Bowery

—

This country-folk song is an apology. We know Taylor loves advising men on handling their relationship issues (for example 'How You Get the Girl'), and forgiveness is another key theme across her catalogue (as in 'Back to December'). The narrative takes place on a front porch – Taylor's favourite place for romantic conversations (as in 'The Last Time'). Here, James explains that he doesn't know much (a response, surely to the repeated refrain of "I knew you" in 'cardigan') and begs for her back.

This is the finale to the Love Triangle trilogy featured across the album. Also spanning 'cardigan' and 'august', the Teenage Love Triangle theory was confirmed by Taylor in the *folklore: Long Pond Studio Sessions* documentary accompanying the album. The three songs all speak of the same period in the trio's lives where they were embroiled in youthful relationships. Taylor imagines an ultimately happy ending for James and Betty, this song's namesake. By spreading their story across three songs, we get to hear multiple perspectives in depth, and build a cinematic universe along the way. 'Betty' feels much more like a teenage romcom than the wistful 'cardigan' and the naïve 'august', demonstrating the nuance and breadth Taylor can convey from one simple story – an impressive feat.

PEACE

WRITERS Taylor Swift, Aaron Dessner

—

Another searing moment of introspection, 'peace' is a song about love and Taylor's own perceived shortcomings in any romance. We see her deliver similarly negative self-evaluations across her catalogue ('Afterglow', 'Anti-Hero'). With Taylor's knack of turning any experience ubiquitous, a song about the impact her fame has on her relationships is also easily interpreted as the perils of being with any partner who is "wild". In 'peace', Taylor is a fire – perhaps the same fire in 'Afterglow' that threatened to destroy them. At odds with the message that she is untameable or in some way "damaged", the song is measured and calm.

 Taylor imagines an ultimately happy ending for James and Betty, this song's namesake

HOAX

WRITERS Taylor Swift, Aaron Dessner

—

Fans and the media like to play detective to try and identify the specific inspirations behind each of Taylor's songs – which she has encouraged with a wealth of Easter eggs. The intentional blending of inspirations in 'hoax' is a new choice for her, encouraged by collaborator Aaron Dessner. Nonetheless, speculation includes specific people across her friendships, relationships and business partners as some of the many sources. It's a song ultimately about betrayal, told across the loose narrative of a one-sided or abusive relationship that the protagonist cannot bring themselves to see with clearer eyes.

THE LAKES

WRITERS Taylor Swift, Jack Antonoff

—

Fame has its benefits, limits, and downsides. In 'the lakes', Taylor begs her lover to sweep her away to England's stunning Lake District so she can forget her problems. She is almost longing to escape to a bygone era and certainly for privacy and the freedom of artistic expression she associates with classic English poets (notably William Wordsworth, who receives a round-about mention in the song). 'The lakes' is a highly referential song, with callbacks to the anniversary meal in 'invisible string', the thief from 'mad woman', and namedropping from 'I Did Something Bad'. This song is the thematic lovechild of 'The Lucky Ones', 'mad woman' and 'I Know Places'.

TOP On stage during the *folklore* set of The Eras Tour.
MIDDLE *Folklore* is one of Taylor's most critically acclaimed albums.
BOTTOM Performing 'betty' with her band and backing singers.

EVERMORE

4 WEEKS AT
NO. **1***

In *folklore*, Taylor established a convincing new direction;
with *evermore*, she completed that arc

WORDS BY DAVE SMITH

WILLOW

WRITERS Taylor Swift, Aaron Dessner

—

This beautifully understated opening track serves two purposes – to let listeners know that Taylor was pursuing the same musical direction as the previous album, *folklore*, and also to emphasise that album's sisterly relationship with *evermore*. Described by Taylor as resembling a "love spell", the lyrics are chanted, low in register and stuffed full of vivid imagery, as well as the excellent observation "I come back stronger than a 90s trend". A surprise release that dominated the upper sections of charts worldwide, *evermore*'s lead single was shortly followed by various remixes, including the 'dancing witch' version by Elvira.

Spotlight on...

CHAMPAGNE PROBLEMS

SEE PAGE 91.

GOLD RUSH

WRITERS Taylor Swift, Jack Antonoff

—

Among the more upbeat offerings on the album, in 'gold rush' the narrator daydreams about the object of her affection, but ultimately decides against pursuing someone so desirable. In many ways, it can be considered a more mature and reflective sister song to 'Gorgeous', where the "beautiful" person in question inspires a mix of jealousy, anxiety and insecurity. Here, the narrator snaps herself out of the daydream, deciding to keep the relationship a fantasy rather than face the potentially disappointing reality.

'TIS THE DAMN SEASON

WRITERS Taylor Swift, Aaron Dessner

—

The entire *evermore* album is a masterclass in economical songwriting where a bare minimum of instrumentation allows the lyrics to breathe, but here's where that art is most evident. In ''tis the damn season', Taylor tells a compact tale of Dorothea (as we learn later on the album) who heads to their hometown for the holidays, either inviting a brief hookup or actually having one with an unnamed former lover (the narrator of 'dorothea'). The emotional kick comes when the narrator reveals that deep down she would prefer to stay with him, instead of returning to her fake life with her equally fake friends in Los Angeles, but has to leave regardless.

TOP Performing the witchy 'willow' on The Eras Tour.
MIDDLE On stage with Aaron Dessner and Jack Antonoff.
BOTTOM At the Rock & Roll Hall of Fame Ceremony in 2021.

TOP The *evermore* Eras set is suitably captivating and emotional.
MIDDLE Taylor "couldn't stop writing songs" after *folklore*.
BOTTOM With the Haim sisters performing 'no body, no crime'.

TOLERATE IT

WRITERS Taylor Swift, Aaron Dessner

—

Follow the time signature of 'tolerate it' if you can – it's either in 10/8 or 5/4, depending on who you ask – and note that Taylor navigates it with ease, telling the story of a woman who feels that her partner barely acknowledges her presence. For this narrative, Taylor was inspired by the 1938 novel *Rebecca* by Daphne du Maurier, in which a relationship between spouses of significantly different ages leads to dissatisfaction. The question that both the novel and the song ask is whether such a situation should be accepted or dissolved through action, with neither work offering us a clear answer.

> *'Happiness' is another song about an imploding relationship, but one that promises redemption as much as detailing heartbreak*

NO BODY, NO CRIME (FEAT. HAIM)

WRITERS Taylor Swift

—

Inspired by Taylor's love of TV crime dramas, this is a murder ballad delivered in a pleasant country-rock style with the assistance of two members of HAIM on backing vocals. A witty, if dark, tale of a homicidal, unfaithful husband whose wife's friends take vengeance on him, 'no body, no crime' spins on the double meaning of the title. First, Taylor speculates that said cheating spouse can't be found guilty because there's no concrete evidence of his infidelity; later, after he's been dispatched by his late wife's vengeful allies, they can't be arrested for the very same reason. It's a lightweight bit of music bearing a heavyweight lyric, and highly enjoyable.

HAPPINESS

WRITERS Taylor Swift, Aaron Dessner

—

Musically, 'happiness' is as stripped-down as any other song from this album, building up at its most raucous only to a droned wash of sweet chords. Lyrically, it's one of the most advanced pieces that Taylor has written, combining stark images from the gothic-literature canon and telling a tale that is both contradictory and persuasive. It's another song about an imploding relationship, for sure, but one that promises redemption as much as detailing heartbreak. One of its key questions is what you do when a good person hurts you; another is what you have left to give when you've already given someone everything.

Spotlight on...
CHAMPAGNE PROBLEMS

WRITERS Taylor Swift, William Bowery

'Champagne problems' is another unhurried, thoughtful tale of love lost. The lyrical twist this time is that the parting of the unnamed lovers in the song is not done on equal terms. The partner, confident that the relationship is secure, is excited to propose, but gets blindsided when Taylor's narrator turns them down. The song also implies that the narrator has mental health issues, something that others judge her for and use to explain away her rejection.

There are thematic similarities to 'Back to December', but here the narrator appears to be somewhat less regretful of her decision, perhaps more akin to 'Midnight Rain'. She knew that rejecting the proposal was the right thing to do, even if she couldn't articulate why to provide closure for her partner.

The piano-led ballad became one of *evermore*'s most popular tracks among critics and fans alike. For such a heartbreaking song, it became an unconventional stadium crowd-pleaser during The Eras Tour, with Taylor explaining how "cathartic" she felt the song would be to sing live. Audiences certainly agree: the performance often earns her a rapturous, minutes-long standing ovation.

The Eras *evermore* dresses include designs in orange, yellow and burgundy.

DOROTHEA

WRITERS Taylor Swift, Aaron Dessner

—

Dorothea is the character that we first met in ''tis the damn season' – a brand-led celeb who lives a plastic life in the artificial world of Los Angeles and connects briefly with a lover on a hometown visit. In this song, Dorothea's partner calls her back, pleading with her to give up her city life and return to country idyll, possibly in the Mississippi town of Tupelo (perhaps significantly, the birthplace of Elvis Presley) that is mentioned in the lyrics. It's a mildly energetic song, with some funky piano here and there, as well as a hooky "ooh, ooh!" that introduces each chorus.

CONEY ISLAND (FEAT. THE NATIONAL)

WRITERS Taylor Swift, William Bowery, Aaron Dessner, Bryce Dessner

—

This understated duet between Taylor and The National's Matt Berninger sees the pair lamenting the loss of a relationship that was taken for granted. There are similarities to the conversational nature of *folklore*'s 'exile', but here our couple are apologetic rather than accusatory. Berninger said that singing with Taylor had been "like dancing with Gene Kelly", and Swift herself was also thrilled with the collaboration. She particularly enjoyed having Berninger – one of her favourite singers – wish her happy birthday in the lyrics, as *evermore* came out just before she turned 31. "That's the real win," she joked.

Spotlight on...

IVY

SEE PAGE 94.

COWBOY LIKE ME

WRITERS Taylor Swift, Aaron Dessner

—

This is a whimsical return to Taylor's roots with a country-folk arrangement. Here, she tells the tale of two "cowboys" – or, in this case, con artists – who have spent their lives swindling unsuspecting victims out of their money by pretending to love them. When this pair of like-minded rogues cross paths, they initially try to play each other, but end up falling in love. After years of chasing material wealth, the couple ultimately find happiness in their relationship. The notion that true love is not materialistic has been explored throughout Taylor's catalogue, but this evocative outlaw narrative gives it a unique spin.

Images: Getty Images.

TOP Eras fans light up their phones in tribute during 'marjorie'.
MIDDLE Pictured at the BRIT Awards in 2021.
BOTTOM Announcing *evermore*, Taylor said "I loved the escapism I found in these imaginary/not imaginary tales".

Spotlight on...
IVY

WRITERS Taylor Swift, Aaron Dessner, Jack Antonoff

This persuasive track is based on the excellent metaphor of ivy, growing unstoppably on a house, as the love of a partner which grows on you – although it may not be desirable for anyone that it does so. The married narrator finds herself entwined with another man, afraid of what will happen if her husband finds out, but nonetheless feels powerless to call off the affair, having fallen in love.

Musically, 'ivy' surges subtly beneath the vocals rather than pushing to the surface, and it's all the better for that because there's a lot of words for Taylor to sing here, as well as a couple of melodic hooks that bring the listener in.

What's really interesting about this song is that it takes an unexpected turn at its midpoint, not dramatically but in an understated way. It could perfectly well have ended before the line "So yeah, it's a war" and been another charming ballad. Instead, its intensity grows from this point, partly because the lyrics become more confrontational and partly because a new, ascending chord sequence begins, pulling us into the story. That's great songwriting – using musical tools, production expertise and lyrical skill to make a song more compelling; 'ivy' goes from a good song to a great one at that point.

LONG STORY SHORT

WRITERS Taylor Swift, Aaron Dessner

—

Lyrically optimistic and musically upbeat, 'long story short' arrives like a refreshing interlude amid *evermore*'s predominantly soft tones. While most of the album explores fictional narratives, this song appears to be based on Taylor's personal experiences, as she reflects on her mid-2010s turmoil with a more relaxed perspective. In a similar vein to the later 'You're on Your Own, Kid', she speaks directly to her younger self, telling past Taylor not to worry about all the drama, because ultimately she will get through it, and will find success, happiness and stability on the other side.

EVERMORE (FEAT. BON IVER)

WRITERS Taylor Swift, William Bowery, Justin Vernon

—

The standard edition of *evermore* closes on a suitably epic note: a piano ballad absolutely stuffed with melodic hooks in the vocals from Taylor and Bon Iver's Justin Vernon. While the latter's high-pitched emoting might be an acquired taste for some, there's no denying that the two voices work perfectly together, and there's a very cool switch in key and tempo in the midsection to keep us on our toes. The song and its narrative evolve together: starting from a sense of hopelessness, rising slowly, coasting effortlessly along in its midsection and then taking a slow dive through the outro to sign off with a glimmer of hope.

> " *You can reasonably speculate that it must be a source of great regret to Taylor that, having inspired her granddaughter to be a singer, her grandmother Marjorie didn't live to see that happen* "

MARJORIE

WRITERS Taylor Swift, Aaron Dessner

—

Warning – this one is a heartbreaker. A sweet tribute to Taylor's late grandmother Marjorie Finlay (1928-2003), this song expresses most of the things that any of us would wish to say to our departed loved ones, if we only could. An especially poignant moment comes when the narrator tells Finlay that she's still alive in her head, but that she wishes she'd been able to know her better. You can reasonably speculate that it must be a source of great regret to Taylor that, having inspired her granddaughter to be a singer, her grandmother didn't live to see that happen, passing away only a decade or so before Taylor became one of the world's biggest-ever artists.

RIGHT WHERE YOU LEFT ME

WRITERS Taylor Swift, Aaron Dessner

—

Sometimes bonus tracks contain unexpected gold, and that's the case with this evocative, surprisingly bitter tale of a spurned lover who is unable to move on – and remains, physically and mentally frozen, waiting for her beau to return. The music is stirring but remains in service to the lyrics and also to Taylor's fantastic melodies, which see her drag the word "I" out to four syllables. The spiralling notes behind the line "You left me, you left me no, you left me no, you left me no choice" will not be forgotten quickly by anyone with a heart. The concepts of denial and being unable to accept reality were explored again in *The Tortured Poets Department*, notably on 'I Hate It Here'.

CLOSURE

WRITERS Taylor Swift, Aaron Dessner

—

Industrial beats open this song, itself based on an odd time signature, and as such it's a satisfyingly weird way to approach the end of the *evermore* album. 'Closure' is a tale of the bitterness, guilt and hypocrisy that comes with the end of a relationship, and therefore not what you'd call a cheerful listen, but come on, if you're going to discuss the ins and outs of human closeness in detail as forensic as Taylor does, you need to cover all the angles, from the good to the grim. Vocally and musically, this song is about as far from the usual Swift approach as you can get, illustrating the breadth of her writing yet again.

IT'S TIME TO GO

WRITERS Taylor Swift, Aaron Dessner

—

This is a simple song with a strong central message – that sometimes quitting a situation and walking away from it is the best course of action, even when doing so is difficult. We can all apply this maxim to any number of lifetime predicaments, and while Taylor doesn't relate it in the lyrics to any recognisable situation from her personal life, you might reasonably speculate that it's about a doomed relationship. The music, as you would expect from everything that's gone before, is calm, understated and designed to support the melodic content rather than make a grand statement.

ALBUM 10 ✦ 21 OCT 2022

MIDNIGHTS

6 WEEKS AT NO. **1***

Taylor delves deep into her insecurities and fantasies
for her tenth album, inspired by "sleepless nights"

WORDS BY FARRAH FROST

LAVENDER HAZE

WRITERS Taylor Swift, Jack Antonoff, Zoë Kravitz, Mark Spears, Jahaan Sweet, Sam Dew

—

Disregarding other people's thoughts on her relationship is by now a very familiar topic for Taylor. She wants to avoid the scrutiny and instead stay cocooned in the hazy, beautiful feeling of their romance. This track appears to address the rumour that she and then partner Joe Alwyn were secretly married, noting a particular misogyny in the assumption. In her Instagram series of song introductions, Taylor likens the pressures of fame to the pressures of social media, connecting her experience to a more relatable one. The dreamy production gives the impression of Swift in the throes of the honeymoon period.

MAROON

WRITERS Taylor Swift, Jack Antonoff

—

It seems it is a lifelong ambition of Taylor's to correctly identify the exact colour of love. Previous songs have coloured it blue, red, and golden. In 'Maroon', Taylor reminisces about a lost relationship, noting all the various shades of red their love was. From flushed cheeks, love bites, and lips, she settles on the titular darker shade. This song is the sultry, darker sister to 'Red': where passion doesn't cloud her evaluation as much – Taylor indirectly confirmed this herself when she 'liked' a fan's TikTok connecting the two songs.

Spotlight on...

ANTI-HERO

SEE PAGE 98.

SNOW ON THE BEACH (FEAT. LANA DEL REY) ⭐

WRITERS Taylor Swift, Lana Del Rey, Jack Antonoff

—

Taylor has high praise for Lana Del Rey, calling her "the most influential artist in pop" and a "legacy" artist. The pair collaborated on 'Snow on the Beach', a song about the rare and beautiful realisation that the person you love is falling for you too. Despite Del Rey being "all over" the original with seamlessly blended vocals throughout, the song was criticised for her seemingly sparse inclusion in the duet. In response, Taylor said "you asked, we listened" and released a 'More Lana Del Rey' version on the album's *Til Dawn* and *Late Night* deluxe editions.

TOP Taylor announced *Midnights* at the VMAs in 2022.
MIDDLE Performing 'Lavender Haze' on The Eras Tour.
BOTTOM With Lana Del Rey at the 2024 Grammy Awards.

Spotlight on...
ANTI-HERO

WRITERS Taylor Swift, Jack Antonoff

—

Taylor once described 'Anti-Hero' as the most honest song she'd written. It's a self-assessment that is critical of her inability to grow, her inevitable repeated return to crisis – and how this essentially makes her unlovable. This is familiar ground for Taylor, who shares her fears of never making meaningful connections last ('peace', for example).

The song explores a number of scenarios where Swift is too big, too complex, too self-involved to ever find happiness. Rather than picturing herself as the underdog as she has done elsewhere (such as 'Long Live'), Taylor's success and personality are instead described in more withering terms. It contains some of her most humorous lyrics: the dramatic reading of her will, the confounding "sexy" baby, the shot taken at sleazy politicians. Notably, the chorus twists an insult that was a common criticism of Taylor's perceived inability to maintain a relationship – she is the problem. Hi.

Despite the self-deprecating message, the song has performed incredibly well both critically and commercially. It broke records for most first-day plays ever on Spotify in 2022, became Taylor's ninth and longest running No. 1 single, and scored multiple nominations and wins across the Grammy, MTV Music Video, BRIT, and iHeartRadio award ceremonies.

LEFT A 'Midnight Rain' performance from The Eras Tour.
RIGHT The iconic burlesque chair-ography from 'Vigilante Shit'.

YOU'RE ON YOUR OWN, KID

WRITERS Taylor Swift, Jack Antonoff

—

Through a series of autobiographical vignettes, Taylor reminisces on a series of events in her life that proved to her that she had to make it alone. It serves as a neat summary of her lyrical abilities: hidden song references, shocking honesty, as the classic Swiftian plot twist. The loneliness of the song's repeated refrain is flipped on its head to become a self-empowering encouragement in the last moment. It's a marked development for Taylor – a comfort and confidence-boosting single that we've never seen from her previously. It is also, of course, the song that launched a million friendship bracelets, which became a fan tradition throughout The Eras Tour.

MIDNIGHT RAIN

WRITERS Taylor Swift, Jack Antonoff

—

The distorted vocals and synthy, woozy production of 'Midnight Rain' sets an atmospheric backdrop to the story of Taylor choosing her career over her partner. While she is making her own name, he is trying to get her to take his in marriage – a change from the declaration in 'Don't Blame Me' that he could decide her name. Rather than the mournful apologetic tone from 'peace', we see the newfound confidence in singledom of 'You're on Your Own Kid' starting to shine through. Rain imagery has often represented romance for Taylor – 'Sparks Fly', for example – but here it is used to symbolise the differences between herself and her sunny partner, who had opposing ideas of where the relationship was heading.

QUESTION...?

WRITERS Taylor Swift, Jack Antonoff

—

'Question…?' has the drunken, loosely confrontational feel of having a (hypothetical?) late-night conversation with an ex-partner things didn't end well with. The first verse recollects the start and end of their relationship, including that much searched for colour of love ('Red', 'illicit affairs', 'daylight'.), We then barrel into the series of questions, interrogating the ex about whether things are as good with his new partner as they were with Taylor. The reverb emphasises key moments in the song, the "oh?" interjecting each line in the chorus, the suitability of his new relationship, and we end on a simple, shrugged shoulder of a line.

VIGILANTE SHIT

WRITERS Taylor Swift

—

Taylor performs her civic duty in 'Vigilante Shit': describing her superhero-like moves that are mostly driven by revenge. Almost certainly inspired by her feud with Scooter Braun over her song ownership, this track sees Taylor taking credit for his downfall. The bridge takes an imperious tone and alludes to the misogyny discussed in 'mad woman'. Taylor is done playing missus nice guy. In an especially popular performance, 'Vigilante Shit' on The Eras Tour is accompanied by a *Chicago The Musical*-inspired dance from *La La Land* choreographer Mandy Moore. It's decidedly more provocative than Taylor's typical performance, showing perhaps that revenge is a dish best served hot.

BEJEWELED

WRITERS Taylor Swift, Jack Antonoff

—

This is a confident, empowering track that reassures us that she will not allow her shine to be dulled. It seems Taylor has two alternative opinions of herself: that she is an unlovable problem ('Anti-Hero'), and that she is a glittering powerhouse ('ME!'). 'Bejeweled' is seemingly her declaration of choosing her career over a life of fragile privacy, "reclaiming" her status as a global figure. Her Easter-egg-adorned music video inverts the classic *Cinderella* fairytale. The song's performance at The Eras Tour includes a dance move – a strut ending with shimmering jazz hands – that she took from a fan's viral video on TikTok, much to that fan's delight.

SWEET NOTHING

WRITERS Taylor Swift, William Bowery

—

'Sweet Nothing' is William Bowery's (the pseudonym of ex-partner Joe Alwyn) final musical contribution to Taylor's catalogue. The soft, simple ballad sits apart from the rest of *Midnights'* heavy synth, instead using an acoustic sound. This, alongside the tender lyrics, gives the track a particularly intimate feel. Though the song is outwardly romantic – with the joys of a mundane and quiet love being celebrated again (a frequent idea for Taylor, as in 'New Year's Day' among others) – given the songwriters' eventual breakup, fans claim the song has taken on new meaning: the "nothing" they once celebrated underpins the eventual demise of their relationship.

> " *Taylor reignited an old fan theory: that she secretly recorded and scrapped an album called* Karma "

LABYRINTH

WRITERS Taylor Swift, Jack Antonoff

—

This is a song about falling in love dangerously fast. Taylor begins the song in the depths of a heartbreak, so when a new love appears she is nervous about trusting it. The distortion of her own voice as a backing vocal becomes something of a trademark for *Midnights*, featuring on 'Midnight Rain' and 'Dear Reader', possibly reflecting the more vulnerable inner voice we hear through the album. The internal monologue of the "breathe in, breathe through, breathe deep, breathe out" advice in the opening verse was actually teased before *Midnights* was even announced: the line features in her New York University commencement speech she gave after receiving an honorary Doctorate of Fine Arts in May 2022.

MASTERMIND

WRITERS Taylor Swift, Jack Antonoff

—

'Mastermind' inverts the perception Taylor often perpetuates about herself: that she is a naïve, helpless romantic at the mercy of destiny ('invisible string', for example). This song flips that narrative and positions Taylor as the architect of her life and relationships. She has talked about planning her moves in 'I Think He Knows' and 'The Man' on *Lover*, and 'Mastermind' gives her a self-confessed "Machiavellian" role of forcing fate's hand. The Swiftian plot twist at the end: that the object of her affection has known all along. Fans also interpret it as her love of plotting meticulous Easter eggs across videos, public appearances, the timing of releases, and more, fuelling even more attention and glory. 'Mastermind' indeed.

KARMA (FEAT. ICE SPICE)

WRITERS Taylor Swift, Jack Antonoff, Mark Spears, Jahaan Sweet, Keanu Torres (and Isis Gaston, Ephrem Lopez on the remix)

—

When Taylor announced this track title, she reignited an old fan theory: that she secretly recorded and scrapped an album called *Karma*. Whether this is true or not remains a mystery, but 'Karma' the song is very much real. It acts as a warning to those who wronged her, and explores the variety of ways in which karma has benefitted her. The single remix also features Ice Spice, who contributed a new verse and raps across the track. On tour, she has occasionally swapped a lyric from the man on the "screen" to "Chiefs", referencing Travis Kelce's football team.

THE GREAT WAR

WRITERS Taylor Swift, Aaron Dessner

—

Taylor often reviews her relationship's arguments in song, such as in 'The Way I Loved You', 'We Are Never Ever Getting Back Together', and 'Afterglow'. In 'The Great War', we seem to be reviewing a fight about a seemingly baseless accusation of infidelity. They ultimately survive, which Taylor takes as a sign that they'll be able to make it through anything. The war theme is underpinned by a military-tinged drumline and lyrics packed with battle references: the soldier, the bloodshed, the poppy. Taylor's previous experiences of cheating have made her a defensive and suspicious partner – something she forewarns in 'The Archer'.

Ice Spice joined Taylor on several Eras Tour dates to perform 'Karma' together.

Taylor was inspired after hearing the phrase "lavender haze" on *Mad Men*.

BIGGER THAN THE WHOLE SKY

WRITERS Taylor Swift

—

Although the song is open to the interpretation that it is about any great loss or bereavement, it is widely speculated that it centres on the story of a miscarriage, although this remains unconfirmed by Taylor. The gentle melody and emotional delivery of the song give the mournful, breathy atmosphere of grief. Lyrically soft and disbelieving, Taylor sings of the life that should've been, of the missed potential and sadness. The song was performed live at The Eras Tour in November 2023 during the Acoustic set, likely in tribute to the Brazilian fan Ana Clara Benevides who tragically passed away after attending her concert in Rio de Janeiro.

PARIS

WRITERS Taylor Swift, Jack Antonoff

—

Once again, Taylor uses fantasy and imagination to symbolise the magic of her romance. In 'Paris', we begin with a 'We Are Never Ever Getting Back Together'-style gossip-fuelled opener, which Taylor ultimately disregards because she is so busy being in love. Paris, often thought of as the "city of love" doesn't even need to be the physical location of her love story, because that is where it transports her to mentally, such is its magic. It revisits the importance of privacy in her relationships, and is possibly a happier counterpart to 'I Know Places' – here the 'places' in question don't even have to be physical.

 There's the classic Swiftian skill of building a whole world in simple lyrics

HIGH INFIDELITY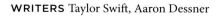

WRITERS Taylor Swift, Aaron Dessner

—

'High Infidelity' delivers much of its context in couplets, a technique honed in 'It's Nice to Have a Friend'. There's the classic Swiftian skill of building a whole world in simple lyrics (the knife-like fences skewer the married suburban fantasy, for example). The "count" being kept seems to callback to the enamoured 'So It Goes…'. The song also mentions a specific date, which sleuths have tried to link to some real-life event, with the prevailing yet unconfirmed theories being that it is the night she met her former partner Joe Alywn, or the night she revealed her role in the Calvin Harris song 'This Is What You Came For'.

TOP On stage in Houston, Texas, in April 2023.
MIDDLE At the Toronto International Film Festival in 2022.
BOTTOM Performing at the Nashville Songwriter Awards where Taylor was named Songwriter-Artist of the Decade.

LEFT Taylor at the AMAs in 2022 where she won six awards including Artist of the Year.
RIGHT 'Karma' closes The Eras Tour shows with a celebratory party.

GLITCH ⭐

WRITERS Taylor Swift, Jack Antonoff, Mark Spears, Sam Dew

'Glitch' tracks Taylor's disbelief that a friendship turned into a genuine romance. The glitch in question is some mistake in the greater plan – another reference to fate, albeit one where fate is trumped by some "malfunction". It's a direct contradiction to 'Mastermind': in 'Glitch' this is a friendship that shouldn't have amounted to anything more. In an early *Midnights* Easter egg, Taylor hinted at the song's title and theme in a TikTok posted in 2021 where the camera literally glitches between scenes. The video was posted a full year before the release of *Midnights*, proving you can never look too far back for clues to her upcoming projects.

DEAR READER ⭐

WRITERS Taylor Swift, Jack Antonoff

Here, Taylor warns us (the "reader") of the perils of following her advice. It is inspired by newspaper advice columns, yet references to drunkenness imply this is that same writer intoxicated by the wasted potential of their own life: their advice is not to be trusted. There's a connection to be made here to 'Anti-Hero': it seems Taylor has almost surpassed being capable of finding true love, in part due to her success. The lyrics also imply how Taylor struggles with being a role model, worrying that she's not worthy of being so idolised. The woozy, distorted, fading-out finale balances her contradiction, alternating between warning us away and reminding us of her appeal.

WOULD'VE, COULD'VE, SHOULD'VE ⭐

WRITERS Taylor Swift, Aaron Dessner

Rife with religious imagery, the lyrics of this track are damning. It takes an unflinching look at the regrets and inequality in a past relationship – with demands placed on possession of Taylor's 'girlhood', accusations of erasure, and overall faux sympathy for the "promising grown man" in question. We have familiar references to Taylor's innocence, and while she admits that there were positives to the relationship, he ultimately had the upper hand. Despite all of this, the regrets feel fresh. Given the reference to being 19 years old during their relationship, fans assume it is rooted in her relationship with John Mayer. This follow-up to the self-confessed "most scathing" of Taylor's songs, 'Dear John', is equally as searing.

HITS DIFFERENT ⭐

WRITERS Taylor Swift, Jack Antonoff, Aaron Dessner

Originally an exclusive track to retailer Target, 'Hits Different' was later included on the *Midnights (Til Dawn Edition)* release and put on streaming services due to fan demand. It almost feels like the narrative precursor to 'Question…?' as it takes place after a tough breakup – more devastating than any she has experienced before – and has a more explicitly intoxicated undercurrent. Self-referential as ever, the movie imagery (the "main guy" is "killed off") connects to 'If This Was a Movie', the idea of being institutionalised links to 'champagne problems' and 'Fortnight', and she takes a drunken taxi ride like in 'Cruel Summer'. The song is a perfect summary of the bewildering, humiliating aftermath of being dumped.

Spotlight on...
YOU'RE LOSING ME

WRITERS Taylor Swift, Jack Antonoff

Opening on a weary sigh, and the sound of her own heartbeat (à la 'Wildest Dreams'), 'You're Losing Me' is a frank and exhausted plea to her lover: she warns him that his actions are causing her to fade away. The simplicity of the lyrics adds to their underlying sadness: she can feel this love slipping through their fingers. The song incorporates medical metaphors – perhaps inspired by Taylor's love of hospital drama *Grey's Anatomy* – likening the relationship to a sick and dying patient with no hope of resuscitation.

A key question from fans was: when was this written? It was listed as a 'From the Vault' track, and – as it came out before her relationship with Alywn had been publicly confirmed as being over – they struggled to identify its inspiration. Helpfully, Jack Antonoff posted on Instagram to share a behind-the-scenes photograph of the day it was written, including a date that placed the track's origins firmly in 2021, several years before Taylor and Joe went their separate ways. Regardless, some fans view the song as autobiographical (inferring that perhaps the couple experienced issues long before their split) and for many it secures *Midnights*' status as a break-up album.

'You're Losing Me' came as a surprise to fans: it first appeared exclusively on sale at specific New York dates of The Eras Tour in 2023, and was eventually released to the wider public in celebration of her being named Spotify's Global Artist in the same year.

THE TORTURED POETS DEPARTMENT

ENTERED AT
NO.1*

This surprise double album brings us over two hours of
captivating narratives with revived self-awareness and wit

WORDS BY FARRAH FROST

Album Artwork: Republic Records. Images: Getty Images. *Source: Billboard 200, correct as of 2 May 2024.

FORTNIGHT (FEAT. POST MALONE)

WRITERS Taylor Swift, Jack Antonoff, Austin Post

——

The opening track and lead single acts as a prologue to the narrative we unravel across the album. Indeed, the whole album could be summed up with the lyric "I love you, it's ruining my life". The song explores the two-week period that changes the protagonist's love life trajectory: a temporary affair that amounted to nothing and alters her brain chemistry. 'Fortnight' foreshadows many other moments from the rest of the album (we move to Florida, develop alcoholism, ghost one another), and Taylor commented that the accompanying music video also visually references many "corners" of the album.

THE TORTURED POETS DEPARTMENT

WRITERS Taylor Swift, Jack Antonoff

——

The title track is a self-deprecating look at an unlikely romance. Taylor fondly mocks her lover – assumed to be based on ex-partner Matty Healy – with hollow laughs and a warmth. It's ultimately not complimentary to either party involved as she recognises the madness and toxicity in their relationship and the performative manner of their artistic process. The iconic poet Dylan Thomas and musician Patti Smith are repeatedly name-dropped: Taylor thinks her lover has delusions of grandeur about their romance and the art they're creating by being together, yet she is in love with him anyway.

> *'Fortnight' foreshadows many other moments from the rest of the album*

MY BOY ONLY BREAKS HIS FAVORITE TOYS

WRITERS Taylor Swift

——

In this synth-pop song, Taylor explains that the reason her partner keeps hurting her is because he really loves her. The song carries a dark message – one of harm and heartbreak – contrastingly told through the infantalising metaphor of a child breaking their toys. After her partner 'breaks' her, he loses interest. Taylor reasons that they're simply, innocently, destructive by nature. It's a common idea associated with toxic relationships – that true love is often painful – and one Taylor has explored before when featuring on the Big Red Machine track 'Renegade'. However, in this song she is so in denial about the reality of this relationship that she believes *she* is the one who needs fixing.

TOP Post Malone collaborated with Taylor on *TTPD*'s lead single.
MIDDLE Taylor surprised fans by making this a double album.
BOTTOM Florence Welch of Florence + The Machine joined Taylor on 'Florida!!!'.

Some fans think
Taylor's preppy,
'dark academia'
looks were teasing
this album.

DOWN BAD

WRITERS Taylor Swift, Jack Antonoff

—

In 'Down Bad', Taylor likens a short-lived relationship to an alien abduction. She's beamed up and experiences "cosmic love", before being abandoned and left without any answers, while those around her question her sanity. The song's message of heartbreak is set to a catchy chorus with uncharacteristically profanity-laced lyrics. 'Down Bad' captures the bereft feeling of a love ending and the downward spiral of heartbreak: a loss of pride, anger, hopelessness. In a callback to 'New Romantics', she reverses her earlier decision that being stranded is "so romantic", and is left "naked and alone" – stripped away from her usual lyrical uniform of dresses.

FRESH OUT THE SLAMMER

WRITERS Taylor Swift, Jack Antonoff

—

This synth-country-infused track begins with an almost spaghetti western film feel. Taylor describes her previous relationship as jail time: handcuffed to it for years and caged by her partner's feelings, with only a daily hour of "sunshine" – just as prisoners might get an hour of yard time. Now she's served her sentence, Taylor's first call is to an old flame. The track features some of the album's multiple references to weddings, or more specifically the absence of her own wedding. The song stands as a metaphor for a stereotypical "rebound" – and Taylor has used criminal motifs to describe ill-fated relationships before, as in 'Getaway Car'.

> " *Swifties have described 'But Daddy I Love Him'*
> *as a "rebellious sister" of 'Love Story'* "

SO LONG, LONDON

WRITERS Taylor Swift, Aaron Dessner

—

The fifth track on a Swift album comes with the expectation of being an emotional one. Taylor previously explained: "As I was making albums… [I was] putting a very vulnerable, personal, honest, emotional song as track five." 'So Long, London' continues that tradition. It's widely assumed to be inspired by the end of her relationship with Joe Alwyn, the muse for *Lover* and, most pertinently, 'London Boy'. In this ballad, Taylor bids farewell to a love that she had worked for but ultimately couldn't hold together on her own. In callbacks to 'You're Losing Me' and 'Renegade', Taylor talks of his "bluest days" and inadequate proof of love, giving her ultimately no choice but to leave the city and relationship she loved so much.

FLORIDA!!!
(FEAT. FLORENCE + THE MACHINE)

WRITERS Taylor Swift, Florence Welch

—

Taylor describes wanting to escape your life in 'Florida!!!' When asked about the choice of location for the song, she explained that she's watched a lot of crime shows, and the Sunshine State seems to be the place people always go to escape or start over with a new identity. The crimes Taylor and Florence seemingly have been accused of committing are infidelity and even murdering their cheating husbands (reminding us of 'no body, no crime'). Locations carry a lot of meaning for Taylor: the home she's been driven out of is presumed to be a follow-up to 'So Long, London'. Fans also noticed that Florida was the first Eras stop Taylor played after her split from Alwyn went public.

BUT DADDY I LOVE HIM

WRITERS Taylor Swift, Aaron Dessner

—

Quickly securing itself as a fan favourite, 'But Daddy I Love Him' is classic Taylor territory. Swifties have described the track as a "rebellious sister" of 'Love Story', as the song follows the same structure and a similar narrative, this time with an unbridled passion that is felt across the whole album. The story uses typical Taylor motifs of forbidden love, getaway cars, leaving a small town and dresses: albeit all with a stronger feeling of scandal throughout. We reach a wild crescendo in each chorus, where an intentionally precocious Taylor professes her love in a direct reference to an iconic line from Disney's animated classic *The Little Mermaid*.

GUILTY AS SIN?

WRITERS Taylor Swift, Jack Antonoff

—

Taylor has previously used religious imagery in her songs: 'False God' and 'Holy Ground' for example. In 'Guilty as Sin?', she asks the question: if I only *think* of cheating, does that count as a sin? In fourth-wall breaking lines she alludes to the "vaults" (a nod to her re-recorded album 'From the Vault' tracks) and that the public want her "propriety" – predicting her fans' strong reactions when rumours of her relationship with Matty Healy started to appear. The reference to The Blue Nile (Healy's favourite band) supports this theory. She finishes with a different question, asking if she can cry. This song is Taylor exploring what permissions she needs to pursue a love.

LEFT Taylor announced this album while accepting her lucky 13th Grammy trophy.
RIGHT Aaron Dessner reunited with Taylor and Jack Antonoff to write on and produce the album.

WHO'S AFRAID OF LITTLE OLD ME?

WRITERS Taylor Swift

In this ode to feminine anger, Taylor revisits the themes of 'mad woman' with refreshed rage. In a continuation of the prison theme of 'Fresh Out the Slammer' and the rising from the dead of 'Look What You Made Me Do', her ghost rises from gallows and haunts her detractors. She draws a comparison between herself and a trained circus animal that has been subdued and mistreated for our enjoyment. She exacts revenge on them in this confrontational, roaring track as she blames them for making her this way: and exacting a warning not to underestimate her. The track's haunting production and delivery of Taylor's lines heightens its spooky and unsettling narrative.

I CAN FIX HIM (NO REALLY I CAN)

WRITERS Taylor Swift, Jack Antonoff

Another episode of *The Tortured Poet Department*'s spaghetti western: this song feels like it's set in a desert town's saloon bar. Taylor has fallen for the small town's rogue cowboy figure, and despite the warnings, she believes she can change him for the better (employing the common relationship trope of a good girl 'redeeming' a bad boy). Believing that, deep down, the scoundrel has the potential to be a good guy, she is convinced of her "skill set" of reforming men (a callback to turning bad guys good in 'Blank Space'). It isn't until the final line she realises the scale of her mistake with a surprised "woah". It's one of several tracks on the album that explores a toxic relationship.

LOML

WRITERS Taylor Swift, Aaron Dessner

This mournful ballad subverts the phrase "love of my life", naming her partner as the "loss" of her life. It's a classic Taylor lyrical technique, twisting a well-known phrase to give it new meaning. 'Loml' tells the story of a rekindled romance that she now believes should have stayed "buried" as the reunited lover ultimately breaks her heart. The song sets the narrative that Taylor pursued this new relationship on the promise of marriage and children, passion and legends, yet was left hollow and cold. The song evokes feelings of grief, comparing the demise of a relationship to death throughout. On any other Swift album, this could easily have been a 'track five' song, but it faced plenty of tough competition on this deeply personal and vulnerable record.

THE SMALLEST MAN WHO EVER LIVED

WRITERS Taylor Swift, Aaron Dessner

This heartfelt song of disappointment, punctuated by Taylor's audible sighs, is a frustrated message to an ex-lover who abandoned their relationship. Taylor is puzzled by his motivations: was his goal to ruin her life? The bridge is accusatory and angry, demanding answers that won't come (perhaps it will be able to rival 'champagne problems' in the ranks of her cathartic bridges?). The track is widely presumed to have been inspired by her brief relationship with The 1975's frontman Matty Healy, given the timing of the song and references to stage lights, buying of pills, and a suit he wears on tour. 'The Smallest Man Who Ever Lived' is an anthem for the ghosted.

Spotlight on...
I CAN DO IT WITH A BROKEN HEART

WRITERS Taylor Swift, Jack Antonoff

This almost disturbingly upbeat song is the first album's sole chipper offering: at least at first glance. 'I Can Do It With a Broken Heart' may be sonically uplifting, but the lyrics tell another, bleaker, story.

The track acts as a parody, exemplifying its core message: Taylor can act happy, even at her lowest. And she can do it well. It breaks the fourth wall (the song opens with the sound of an "in ear" piece, the equipment an artist uses on stage, and fans at listening parties join in with the fictional crowd shouting "more!"), and is deeply self-aware. It's an almost toxic relationship between her and her audience: when she's at her lowest they are oblivious. Taylor is smiling on demand, isolated among crowds of thousands. The song asks: what happens when you commodify your heartbreak? The answer Taylor lands on is a glittering smile through sometimes gritted teeth.

Despite the different sound, it represents the album's central theme of the conflicts Taylor feels about creating heartbreak art. 'I Can Do It With a Broken Heart' tells us, unequivocally, that we never truly know what's going on in her personal life, and that she can put on a damn good show every single night anyway.

THE ALCHEMY

WRITERS Taylor Swift, Jack Antonoff

—

One of the few happy songs on *The Tortured Poets Department*, 'The Alchemy' is the story of a relationship that was destined to be. Colour is a favourite theme of Taylor's (see 'Red', 'Daylight', 'Maroon'), with alchemy being the art of turning something into gold. Fate in relationships is also common in Taylor's songs (such as 'invisible string' and 'The Story of Us'), here positioned as something that can't possibly be fought against. Given the multiple football references (a new field in Taylor's work) – from touchdowns and winning streaks to leagues and trophies – this song is generally assumed to be inspired by her relationship with American footballer Travis Kelce.

IMGONNAGETYOUBACK

WRITERS Taylor Swift, Jack Antonoff

—

'Imgonnagetyouback' is a wonderfully Swiftian play on words, with an undecided Taylor considering whether to forgive or exact revenge on an ex-lover. Even before its release, the song courted controversy when fans preemptively speculated it was a similar song to Olivia Rodrigo's single 'Get Him Back'. Despite the conceptual similarities, 'imgonnagetyouback' is less anarchistic and more in control than Rodrigo's hit track: Taylor's ex has wanting and remorse in his eyes. The song feels like a narrative follow-up to the character Taylor created in 'Blank Space' – smashing up her lover's vehicles and love being a game they both want to play.

> *Taylor is revisiting old narratives with renewed perspectives*

CLARA BOW

WRITERS Taylor Swift, Aaron Dessner

—

Taylor explores the fickleness of fame in 'Clara Bow'. She's explored fame's downsides in 'Nothing New' and 'The Lucky One', but here she delivers the song from the mouths of her flatterers, who do not hear the foreboding in their praise. Throughout the song she namedrops Clara Bow, the 1920s silent-screen starlet who was institutionalised (including receiving shock therapy, depicted in the 'Fortnight' music video). Stevie Nicks, the 70s music icon is also mentioned: Nicks is an industry legend who has battled with addictions. 'Clara Bow' juxtaposes these compliments with the tragedies of the women it lauds: ending with a pensive assessment of herself.

THE ALBATROSS

WRITERS Taylor Swift, Aaron Dessner

—

Taylor establishes herself as a bonafide poet with literary references flowing through 'The Albatross'. This is a subtle distinction from the characters of earlier song 'The Tortured Poets Department': instead of performativity, Taylor infuses classical poetry knowledge into the song. 'The Albatross' is inspired by the mythical story told in Samuel Coleridge's 1798 poem *The Rime of the Ancient Mariner*. In the poem, a mariner kills the seafaring bird – believing it to be cursed – and is punished for this sin by being forced to wear its carcass around his neck forevermore. Coleridge is a founding member of the Lakes Poets that also inspired Taylor's song 'the lakes'.

THE BLACK DOG

WRITERS Taylor Swift

—

Taylor has written many of her songs about a specific experience in her life that becomes ubiquitous for millions of fans: 'The Moment I Knew' is a disappointing birthday, 'Enchanted' is the first time meeting someone. In this song, Taylor veers from shock, grief and anger when she realises her ex-partner has forgotten to turn his phone's shared location off, meaning she can see he has revisited their old favourite bar without her. This modern heartbreak is as unique as it is relatable. She can't understand how he doesn't miss her the way she misses him – a theme we've seen before in 'All Too Well'. One London pub made headlines after happily finding itself inundated with Swifties, but whether or not it is indeed *the* Black Dog remains unconfirmed.

CHLOE OR SAM OR SOPHIA OR MARCUS

WRITERS Taylor Swift, Aaron Dessner

—

Taylor captures the feeling of 'the one that got away' in this soft and pensive song. There are striking connections to her *folklore* opener 'the 1', reminiscing about a relationship that the participants let drift away. Both songs have a lingering love, a story of moving on, new lovers found via the internet and a recurring question about what could have been – although this song is much more regretful and longing for what once was, with Taylor lacking a sense of closure. It also features a direct callback to her song 'Maroon'; as we see throughout this album, Taylor is revisiting old narratives with renewed perspectives.

Taylor's monochromatic glamour at the 2023 MTV VMAs.

Taylor pictured at the premiere for Beyoncé's *Renaissance* film.

LEFT A portrait of Taylor from the 2024 Grammy Awards.
RIGHT Of all their collaborations, Jack Antonoff said that *TTPD* is his favourite so far.

HOW DID IT END?

WRITERS Taylor Swift, Aaron Dessner

Taylor has often repositioned the tabloid fodder of her global fame as more akin to small-town gossip ('thanK you aIMee') – often from the perspective of someone trying to protect a relationship ('Lavender Haze') or begin one ('End Game'). This song is the imagined conversations of even the most seemingly empathetic of friends who see her heartbreak only as entertainment. This is an overriding theme on the album: her love life and career's apparent incompatibility. Although the scale of the rubbernecking is different for the global stardom of Swift, it's a shared feeling with anyone who has experienced turmoil that has been fuel for gossip.

SO HIGH SCHOOL

WRITERS Taylor Swift, Aaron Dessner

High school is a recurrent setting in Taylor's discography, going right back to songs like 'Fifteen' and 'You Belong With Me'. It isn't always a positive setting – in 'Miss Americana & the Heartbreak Prince' it is somewhere to escape from together – but here we have a rose-tinted view of a youthful, joyous romance. Taylor enjoys a love that undoes all her negative experiences as an adult: this is pure, innocent and uncomplicated. The song feels like we have revisited the hopeful romantic Taylor from *Taylor Swift* or *Fearless*. It's widely believed to be inspired by her relationship with Travis Kelce, playing on the high school tropes of the bookish girl dating the guy on the football team.

I HATE IT HERE

WRITERS Taylor Swift, Aaron Dessner

'I Hate It Here' carries a central theme of the album: Taylor believes that reality is disappointing. She finds her dreams and inner life more fulfilling – the romances of "finance guys" do not impress her, and the games of her friends are no longer fun when she brings her cynicism. She is untrusting of nostalgia and other people, instead preferring to retreat inwards, spending time with her own thoughts and dreams. The book she references is most likely *The Secret Garden* by Frances Hodgson Burnett. This song has been likened by fans to *folklore*'s 'the lakes', another introverted song about escaping to a preferable fantasy world, but this time with more pessimism and aloofness.

THANK YOU AIMEE

WRITERS Taylor Swift, Aaron Dessner

Taylor has only loosely disguised the song's inspiration – despite what she sings in the lyrics – as a "defining clue" is barely hidden in the title. The capitalisation of 'KIM' is surely an all-but-confirmed nod to Kim Kardashian, whom Taylor here describes as akin to a small-town high school bully (in reference to her 2016 feud with Kim and her then husband Kanye West, which ultimately led to Taylor creating *reputation*). As with *Speak Now*'s 'Mean', this thinly veiled critic has wasted their time in trying to bring Taylor down. Here, she has the benefit of perspective: she has built her legacy and understands the role her bully played in motivating Taylor to achieve more.

I LOOK IN PEOPLE'S WINDOWS

WRITERS Taylor Swift, Jack Antonoff, Patrik Berger

In break-up song 'Death By a Thousand Cuts', the character peers through boarded-up windows as a metaphor for yearnful reminiscing. In 'I Look in People's Windows', Taylor refreshes the imagery in more detail. Here, she is searching for any sign of her ex-lover, hoping that one more glimpse of her might inspire him to return to her. Taylor is othered, excluded from the warmth of a home – possibly a thematic connection to the Lover House theory that established her various albums as different rooms in the fictional home that the couple in the 'Lover' music video share. It can also be interpreted as Taylor's sense of being an outsider compared to those inside with their 'normal' lives.

PETER

WRITERS Taylor Swift

A wistful song that recalls the youthful promises of a past love. In 'Peter', Taylor puts herself into the world of J M Barrie's stories of Peter Pan, taking on the role of Wendy returning to reality from Neverland. Wendy is forced to leave the window she waited by for her Peter Pan: he either never came to find her, or did not fulfil his other promise to grow up. This can be interpreted as a partner who was immature, or didn't feel ready for a relationship, but made promises of 'someday'. Taylor is done waiting, and mourns what could have been if he had only kept his promises. It echoes the childhood loves of 'seven', and of course the "Peter losing Wendy" lyric of 'cardigan'.

> **In 'The Manuscript', Taylor captures her artistic process from start to end across her whole career**

THE PROPHECY

WRITERS Taylor Swift, Aaron Dessner

Fate is a recurring motif in Taylor's discography. It's often used to invoke the certainty of a love ('Timeless'), but in 'The Prophecy' she's reduced to begging to change her fate. The song could be read as a wider self-assessment. She describes being cursed, becoming undignified in desperation, watching her failed romances unfold before her. She nods to her riches in the chorus – she'd exchange it all for a love that lasts. It's another of the album's critical introspection songs, in which she infantilises herself ('But Daddy I Love Him'), suffers alone ('I Can Do It with a Broken Heart') or is "deranged" ('I Look in People's Windows').

THE BOLTER

WRITERS Taylor Swift, Aaron Dessner

In this song, Taylor sets the scene with a child who has a near-death drowning experience. Later in life, this character goes on to become afraid of commitment, feeling a similar sense of drowning in relationships and finding relief in fleeing. The image of escape recurs through Taylor's catalogue, and this track seems to nod to many of them: the screeching cars of 'Getaway Car', the taming of men in 'Blank Space', being able to breathe again in 'Clean'. Indeed, the woman in 'The Bolter' seems to be a spiritual sister of the woman in 'Blank Space': they're both hotly pursued lovers, men-manipulators, and serial heartbreakers – except in 'The Bolter', she's the one who leaves.

CASSANDRA

WRITERS Taylor Swift, Aaron Dessner

If the phrase "I told you so" was a song, then this would be it. Another track on the album using literary inspiration, the titular character is the prophet who foresaw the Trojan Horse betrayal in Greek mythology. Cassandra was a prophet doomed never to be believed, and while the song seemingly is inspired by the past feud with Kim Kardashian and Kanye West, it is relatable to anyone who has not been listened to and has had their warnings ignored. The track uses imagery (such as witch burnings and snakes) that we know well from her *reputation* era – the song is 'This Is Why We Can't Have Nice Things' in a more mature guise.

ROBIN

WRITERS Taylor Swift, Aaron Dessner

This sweet ballad crystallises youth. Taylor sings to the titular character, a young child, encouraging them to keep growing, marvelling at their zeal, and admiring their obliviousness to the cruelty of the world. Fans have speculated this could be written to her younger self, to collaborator Aaron Dessner's son Robin (arguably the most likely inspiration), the fictional Christopher Robin from A A Milne's Winnie-the-Pooh series, or even the late actor Robin Williams (who both played Peter Pan and starred in *Dead Poets Society*). This universal sentiment could be any parent protecting and curating their child's world to sustain their innocence and joy for as long as possible.

Spotlight on...
THE MANUSCRIPT

WRITERS Taylor Swift

———

'The Manuscript', acts as a summary of Taylor's career, though fans and publications have also been quick to conclude the track is inspired by particular relationships (most prominent speculation suggests Jake Glyenhall). Taylor writes about her artistic process as a whole: 1: experience a love or a heartbreak, 2: produce art about it that she hands over to others, and in doing so, 3: experience closure.

It seems to be most clearly about the experience of 'All Too Well (Ten Minute Version)': heartbreak turned into handwritten lyrics in her diary – a song too painful to perform live, a persistent fan legend – then eventually into a re-recorded song with all ten minutes and a Golden Globe-nominated short film. She has talked before about how 'All Too Well' has changed for her, now it reminds her of her fans.

She captures her artistic process from start to end across her whole career, with nods to other past muses sprinkled throughout ("sparks" as in 'Sparks Fly', slow dancing as in 'You Are in Love'). On an even wider scale, there is possibly an over-arching theme of her reclaiming her music following her masters disputes. She has fought to re-record her music so that it can truly belong to its rightful owners: us.

THE SINGLES & MORE

Inside the songs that Taylor wrote for non-album projects such as
movie soundtracks – or for the holiday season!

WORDS BY DAVE SMITH

CHRISTMASES WHEN YOU WERE MINE

RELEASED 14 October 2007
FROM *The Taylor Swift Holiday Collection*
WRITERS Taylor Swift, Liz Rose, Nathan Chapman

—

Back in 2007, Taylor released a short-but-sweet six-track Christmas EP, *The Taylor Swift Holiday Collection.* Alongside four covers of classics ('Last Christmas', 'Santa Baby', 'Silent Night' and 'White Christmas'), she also included two of her own festive compositions, which many critics considered to be highlights on the record. The first of this original pair, 'Christmases When You Were Mine', is a bittersweet acoustic-only song, with Taylor delivering nostalgic lines about times past in her charming warble. Even at this early stage, she and her producers evidently understood the value of a stripped-down arrangement and production, something from which other young musicians could well learn.

CHRISTMAS MUST BE SOMETHING MORE

RELEASED 14 October 2007
FROM *The Taylor Swift Holiday Collection*
WRITERS Taylor Swift

—

The second of Taylor's original contributions for *The Taylor Swift Holiday Collection*, this chirpy little tune appears to be a Yuletide thumbs-up to the Messiah ("Here's to the birthday boy who saved our lives") and, like a small piece of Christmas cake, is sweet and tasty without taking up much time and space. Musically, it's a bit of country-pop and not especially Christmassy in tone: you won't hear any sleigh bells here. Indeed, were it not for the seasonal lyrics that teenage Taylor delivers in her sunny, youthful tone, this song could be a fixture at the average Tennessee summer hoedown.

CHRISTMAS TREE FARM

RELEASED 6 December 2019
WRITERS Taylor Swift

—

One of the last cheerful events of the pre-Covid era, 'Christmas Tree Farm' was released in early December 2019 and is a blast from start to finish. Sure, it bears comparison to Mariah Carey's perennial Christmas anthem 'All I Want for Christmas Is You' released 25 years prior, but it's less frenetic and more digestible than that inescapable Yuletide hit. Instead, Taylor reverts to her youthful self, vocally and lyrically at least, delivering lines about the seasonal good times she enjoyed back on the ol' family farm with an unrestrained cheeriness that isn't often heard in her modern songs.

Images: Getty Images.

TOP A festive Taylor collecting toys for charity in 2007.
MIDDLE Performing at the iHeartRadio Z100 Jingle Ball in 2019.
BOTTOM Pictured with her parents, Scott and Andrea. Taylor's "magical childhood" inspired 'Christmas Tree Farm'.

TOP Taylor often made 'heart hands' to fans in her early career.
MIDDLE A portrait from a *Us Weekly* cover shoot in 2008.
BOTTOM Performing at the *TIME* 100 Gala in 2019.

I HEART ?

RELEASED 24 October 2006 | 15 July 2008
FROM *Taylor Swift* download bonus | *Beautiful Eyes* EP
WRITERS Taylor Swift

———

This chirpy bit of bubblegum country-pop is based on a cheerfully ascending chord pattern and is a highlight of the *Beautiful Eyes* EP, released as a stopgap between albums one and two. 'I Heart ?', as you might surmise from its teen-friendly title, was written back in 2003 when Taylor was a mere 14 years old. It served as the perfect promo single for the EP at the time, but listening back to it after all these years is a reminder of just how far she's come: on this song she sings in the high-register voice of a relative youngster, and its subject – a joyous teenage crush – is cute rather than sophisticated. Enjoy this song, it's an innocent blast.

BEAUTIFUL EYES

RELEASED 15 July 2008
FROM *Beautiful Eyes* EP
WRITERS Taylor Swift

———

'Beautiful Eyes' could have been the theme tune to literally any teen drama of the Nineties or Noughties, such is its sweet appeal and hummable melodies. Lyrically, it's more lovelorn-adolescent stuff, of course, but that's absolutely to be expected given the point in Taylor's career when she wrote and released it, and what the heck: if you like honeyed pop with a few twanging guitars to push it along, you'll enjoy it. One second short of three minutes, this song doesn't outstay its welcome, as the best pop songs never do – with country elements or not – and this one seems to come and go before you know it.

ALL OF THE GIRLS YOU LOVED BEFORE

RELEASED 17 March 2023
FROM Outtake from *Lover*, promotional single for The Eras Tour
WRITERS Taylor Swift, Louis Bell, Adam King Feeney

———

An urban ballad with autotuned edges and a very slick production, 'All of the Girls You Loved Before' is proof positive that the R&B world is Taylor Swift's for the taking should she choose to embrace it, the pop arena having been dominated by her music for more than a decade. It's a love song, with the narrator's dedication to its subject refined because of his previous lovers rather than despite them. Sure, it may be a little anodyne in comparison to the pointed, intellectual approach she takes to the nuances of love elsewhere, but as hits go, it does the stadium-filling trick nicely.

Spotlight on...
ONLY THE YOUNG

RELEASED 31 January 2020
FROM Promotional single for *Miss Americana*
WRITERS Taylor Swift, Joel Little

—

Who better to write a song offering succour and support to young people during the Trump regime than Taylor Swift? Released just weeks before the world shut down for two years, 'Only the Young' was a clear statement of fact: that government ("the big bad man and his big bad clan", as she put it, anonymously and wisely) would not triumph over people's civil rights without a fight, and that this fight can and will be won – as long as we don't give up. Taylor, who had refrained in her earlier career from commenting extensively on social issues of most kinds, now elected to support a range of progressive causes, and 'Only the Young' was her way of making this clear.

The title is most revealing. As Taylor undoubtedly knows, youth is essential if serious social change is to take place. Older generations can lack the motivation to push through any revolution, while young people see no barriers whatsoever to doing exactly that. The same young people perceive Taylor's message most clearly, engage best with her music and understand the ideals of *Miss Americana*, the documentary film which 'Only the Young' was released to promote. Most of the young also want a Trump-free future, it should be noted.

YOU'LL ALWAYS FIND YOUR WAY BACK HOME

RELEASED 24 March 2009
FROM *Hannah Montana: The Movie*
WRITERS Taylor Swift, Martin Johnson

—

Written for the massively successful *Hannah Montana* movie of 2008, and released on the soundtrack a year later, this song was co-created by Taylor for the film's star – fellow teen talent, Miley Cyrus – to perform. It's an upbeat pop-rock song with a key-change halfway through, a reliable tool used in songwriting to give a composition an unexpected kick. Note that Swift and Cyrus occupy similar commercial space, three years apart in age and with a country background: this song could have been sung by Taylor herself and been equally popular. It didn't chart highly in 2009, but can you imagine its potential success if either singer re-recorded it nowadays?

CRAZIER

RELEASED 24 March 2009
FROM *Hannah Montana: The Movie*
WRITERS Taylor Swift, Robert Ellis Orrall

—

If you've seen *Hannah Montana: The Movie*, you'll recall the scene when Taylor makes a cameo appearance, singing this song. It's a phones-aloft ballad, with full dimensions that would make it suitable for even the biggest arena, and indeed the guest slot is understandably overshadowed Miley Cyrus' own star role. The track itself is about falling in love with someone who brings joy and wonder back into your life. With its country-pop sensibility, 'Crazier' could have easily fit in on *Fearless*, but there's a different connection to the album: the actor who played Miley's love interest in the film, Lucas Till, went on to star opposite Taylor in the music video for 'You Belong with Me'.

EYES OPEN

RELEASED 27 March 2012 | 17 March 2023 (Taylor's Version)
FROM *The Hunger Games*
WRITERS Taylor Swift

—

Channelling the spirit of Noughties pop-rock – like Paramore, say – this song is a slice of super-catchy rock, expertly anchored by Taylor's own vocal hook and a clutch of chunky guitar riffs. Nothing works better in an arena than a descending chord sequence, and that's exactly what you'll find underneath the chorus, itself a fearsomely melodic repetition of the title that you will be unable to forget once you've heard it. Originally included on the *Hunger Games* soundtrack, 'Eyes Open' was more recently released as part of Taylor's re-recording campaign, and is all the better for it.

I DON'T WANNA LIVE FOREVER (FEAT. ZAYN)

RELEASED 9 December 2016
FROM *Fifty Shades Darker*
WRITERS Taylor Swift, Sam Dew, Jack Antonoff

—

This slick chunk of electro-pop, R&B balladry proves that Taylor can occupy more or less any musical territory with consummate ease, her vocals sliding pleasantly under those of the former One Direction singer Zayn Malik. The sultry song finds the narrators separately agonising over their past relationship, wishing they could be together again. The track placed Taylor at the forefront of commercial music, exposing her to the affluent *Fifty Shades* demographic at the same time. It has to be said that Zayn's falsetto squeals aren't for everyone, giving the impression that he's stuck in a lift with a boa constrictor, but that didn't stop his fans from snapping this single up.

BEAUTIFUL GHOSTS

RELEASED 15 November 2019
FROM *Cats*
WRITERS Taylor Swift, Andrew Lloyd Webber

—

The *Cats* movie of 2019 was tedious, incomprehensible and wholly embarrassing for everyone who appeared in it – except for Taylor Swift. This may be because she performed a masterful rendition of 'Macavity' and was given a non-ridiculous CGI makeover, but it also helped that she co-wrote this great song for the soundtrack. Taylor saves the day, as she pretty much always does, with a beautiful vocal performance that complements the accompanying piano and strings perfectly. The other writer is Andrew Lloyd Webber, which means that it's as lovey as only musical theatre can be ("I feel so alive!"), but come on, who doesn't love all those overblown sentiments?

CAROLINA

RELEASED 24 June 2022
FROM *Where the Crawdads Sing*
WRITERS Taylor Swift

—

Olivia Newman's 2022 film adaptation of *Where the Crawdads Sing* is a thoughtful, textured production, and this song from its soundtrack emulates those qualities, remaining downbeat for most of its four and a half minutes. There's a break and a resurgence near the end, so it isn't completely without dynamics, but most of the song is made up of Taylor's vocal lament and a strummed guitar accompaniment. It might be a bit of a stretch to invoke the name of the godfather of the modern murder ballad, Nick Cave, but 'Carolina' definitely nods towards that darkest of all dark territories.

Spotlight on...

SAFE & SOUND

(FEAT. THE CIVIL WARS)

RELEASED 26 December 2011 | 17 March 2023
(Taylor's Version)
FROM *The Hunger Games*
WRITERS Taylor Swift, Joy Williams, John Paul White,
T Bone Burnett

——

Great songwriting is often as much about leaving space
empty as it is about filling it, and there's very little to
this sweet, unhurried folk ballad. What's refreshing
about this is that 'Safe & Sound' was written in 2012
for the soundtrack of a Hollywood tentpole movie, *The
Hunger Games*. While that movie wasn't quite as huge,
commercially speaking, as a Marvel or DC superhero
movie or other mainstream production, it was still a
large-scale release, and films of that size tend to have
pretty unsubtly music to accompany the visuals.

'Safe & Sound' is the polar opposite of unsubtle. There's
no giant build to a power-ballad conclusion; there's
barely any instrumentation, acoustic guitars aside; and
Taylor's vocals are mostly unaccompanied, with a couple
of harmony lines here and there from the Civil Wars, a
Nashville folk duo consisting of Joy Williams and John
Paul White.

The focus of the song lies squarely on Taylor herself,
who excels vocally, delivering ascending melodies of
serious complexity in her upper range. It's something of
a masterclass in vocal skill, and not one we often tend
to hear a decade later, when she tends to employ her
mid- and lower register more frequently. The track was
nominated for several major industry accolades, and
won the Best Song Written for Visual Media at the 2013
Grammy Awards (pictured).

TAYLOR'S COLLABORATIONS

Taylor reserves featured appearances for a very select few: friends and heroes.
When she's extended this to lovers, she has found less favourable outcomes…

WORDS BY FARRAH FROST

TWO IS BETTER THAN ONE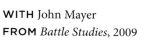

WITH Boys Like Girls
FROM *Love Drunk*, 2009
WRITERS Martin Johnson, Taylor Swift

———

At a time when Taylor was best known for her dominance in the country music genre, it came as a surprise to see her collaborating with emo pop-rock band Boys Like Girls. The song is more delicate than the rest on the *Love Drunk* album, and sets a wistful tone as the protagonist realises that perhaps this romance is worthwhile, given his love's profound impact on him. Co-written by Taylor and the Boys Like Girls lead Martin Johnson, they harmonise together as we hear Taylor's influence on the song: the overriding sense of falling in love.

HALF OF MY HEART

WITH John Mayer
FROM *Battle Studies*, 2009
WRITERS John Mayer

———

This pop-rock duet portrays the duality of a relationship that the lovers are unsure of and can't fully commit to. Taylor's feature on this song became contentious. Despite an original recording featuring her singing across the chorus and bridge, later versions were released without her vocals. Fans believe John Mayer has 'erased' Taylor from the song in retaliation to her music that heavily referenced their soured relationship ('Dear John' is widely believed to be about him). There is also a *Lover* connection in this song's lyrics, with a line describing a wedding with a "paper ring".

> *Taylor and B.o.B meld perfectly together in tone and message*

BOTH OF US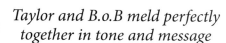

WITH B.o.B
FROM *Strange Clouds*, 2012
WRITERS Bobby Ray Simmons Jr., Taylor Swift, Ammar Malik, Lukasz Gottwald, Henry Walter

———

In this anti-bullying song, Taylor collaborates with B.o.B. The central message is one of empowerment, with Taylor wishing in the chorus that she had the strength to rescue "both of us" from the pressures and circumstances that hold us down. While her chorus and Bobby Ray's verses are sonically set apart, they meld perfectly together in tone and message. Taylor's chorus is simple and sweet, and she makes a childlike promise to someday lift us out of pain. There's a loose connection to 'Mean', where she envisions a brighter future for herself.

TOP On stage in 2009 with Martin Johnson from Boys Like Girls.
MIDDLE Taylor's relationship with John Mayer inspired later songs.
BOTTOM Performing 'Both of Us' with B.o.B in 2012.

TOP On stage with Keith Urban and Tim McGraw in 2013.

MIDDLE Performing 'Big Star' with Kenny Chesney, who appeared as a surprise guest on the Speak Now Tour.

BOTTOM With Calvin Harris at the 2015 *Billboard* Music Awards.

HIGHWAY DON'T CARE

WITH Tim McGraw feat. Keith Urban
FROM *Two Lanes of Freedom*, 2013
WRITERS Mark Irwin, Josh Kear, Brad Warren, Brett Warren

———

This song marked something of a full-circle moment for Taylor: one of her first major breakthrough songs was named after country music hero Tim McGraw, and there she was seven years later collaborating with him. Years later, she completes the set and collaborates with this track's legendary guitarist Keith Urban on 'That's When' for *Fearless (Taylor's Version)*. The song is a classic country ballad, detailing the long drive home of an ex-lover who cannot stop thinking about him. Taylor sings the track's pre-chorus, which acts as the fictional tune on the radio the protagonist hears as she tries to distract herself.

BIG STAR (LIVE)

WITH Kenny Chesney
FROM *Live in No Shoes Nation*, 2017 (recorded 2015)
WRITERS Stephony Smith

———

Although the song was written years before Taylor's rise to fame, it has proven to have had an almost psychic quality. There are a number of references to the shy country girl who believes in her dreams and become a "big star" from a small town. Foreshadowing "fearlessly" hitting highs, not caring about high school bullies (à la 'Mean'), the accusations of promiscuity ('Blank Space') and enjoying the pleasures of fame ('Bejeweled'). Dedicated to "girls with dreams", Taylor needs no introduction as she surprises the crowd by appearing to perform the second verse.

BIRCH

WITH Big Red Machine
FROM *How Long Do You Think It's Gonna Last?*, 2021
WRITERS Aaron Dessner, Bryan Devendorf, Justin Vernon

———

One of several projects with Aaron Dessner, and one of two on Big Red Machine's *How Long Do You Think It's Gonna Last?* album. Some fans speculate that 'Birch' represents a man's perspective in a relationship, while the next Taylor feature 'Renegade' represents the woman's. 'Birch', an intensely intentional song, dismantles and reimagines phrases and drops hyper-specific references like children's names, to give the impression of a man who is not flexible, not graceful, pining and ready for regrowth. Swift's contribution was her vocals, and in an *NME* interview, Aaron confirmed that it was Taylor who came up with the album's title.

Spotlight on...
THIS IS WHAT YOU CAME FOR

WITH Calvin Harris feat. Rihanna
FROM Standalone single, 2016
WRITERS Calvin Harris, Taylor Swift (as Nils Sjöberg)

——

Taylor was not officially on this song – a lovely lyrical piece performed expertly by Rihanna, set to Harris' trademark euro-dance pop. Her backing vocals were uncredited and her pseudonym, Nils Sjöberg, was listed in the writing and production credits. Originally opting for secrecy to avoid any media scrutiny, Taylor didn't want her involvement to overshadow a song she was proud of, but when TMZ revealed the true identity of "Nils" in 2016, she had little choice but to confirm her role on the song.

Her collaborator, and at that point her recent ex-boyfriend, DJ Calvin Harris took to social media to express his anger at the confirmations. In a series of now-deleted posts, he accused Taylor and her team of "going out of their way" to make him look bad. He accused her of looking for "someone to bury" as a promotional tool, and name-dropped Katy Perry as an example of someone she was willing to burn for her own career. The outburst was a contributing factor to Taylor's public fall from grace, and potentially referenced later in the 'I Forgot That You Existed' line "you showed who you are". The gravestone of "Nils Sjöberg" can be seen in the opening scene of music video extravaganza 'Look What You Made Me Do'.

Spotlight on...

THE JOKER AND THE QUEEN

WITH Ed Sheeran
FROM = *(Tour Edition)*, 2022
WRITERS Ed Sheeran, Taylor Swift, Johnny McDaid, Fred Gibson, Sam Roman

———

Taylor and Ed have been friends and collaborators for over a decade. He was one of her support act on the Red Tour, and is featured on both *Red* ('Run' and 'Everything Has Changed'), and *reputation* ('End Game'), making him one of the most prolific featured artist across her discography to date. 'The Joker and the Queen' is the first song of Ed's that Taylor features on.

The collab was initially teased through Easter eggs: carving an equals sign (the album title) into a cake in a scene on the 'I Can See You' music video, and releasing a deck of cards in her merch store in the run up to the song's release. There's also a major *Red* connection in the music video of 'The Joker and the Queen' – the actors who as children played a mini Sheeran and Swift in the video for 'Everything Has Changed' reprised their roles.

The song is a sweet love story, dedicated to Sheeran's wife. In it, she is the "queen" and he the mere "joker" – the song praises her for seeing the positives in him. Despite being largely penned by Ed, it's rife with Swiftian imagery: regality and gambling and finding true love in the simple luxuries.

RENEGADE

WITH Big Red Machine
FROM *How Long Do You Think It's Gonna Last?*, 2021
WRITERS Aaron Dessner, Taylor Swift

——

The counterpart perspective to 'Birch', 'Renegade' explores the at times frustrating experience of trying to love someone who is struggling with their mental health. The song revisits the theme of an unequal relationship, but this time, it is their health and anxiety that are the suspected culprits in tipping the balance. Taylor wants him to get it together, in part for his own benefit, but moreover so he can finally love her as she deserves. Taylor has persevered through the troubles (following her own advice from 'All You Had to Do Was Stay') and is becoming impatient. The song became Big Red Machine's first single to appear in the charts.

GASOLINE

WITH HAIM
FROM *Women in Music Pt. III* expanded edition, 2021
WRITERS Danielle Haim, Este Haim, Alana Haim, Rostam Batmanglij, Ariel Rechtshaid

——

Taylor appears on the remix version of HAIM's hit 'Gasoline' after she told the band it was her favourite song of theirs. As longtime friends, she has collaborated with the Haim sisters several times – they're cast as the 'ugly stepsisters' in her 'Bejeweled' music video retelling of *Cinderella* and appear on *evermore*'s 'no body, no crime'. The song is a slow jam, asserting a woman's control and unmet sexual desires. Taylor's verse adds a new layer to the song, portraying a relationship that is tinged with depression and retaliation. She sings of striking matches and watching them "blow" – either blown out or blown up – alluring in the context of the song's sexual tones.

THE ALCOTT

WITH The National
FROM *First Two Pages of Frankenstein*, 2023
WRITERS Matt Berninger, Aaron Dessner, Taylor Swift

——

Another swift reply from Taylor, Aaron Dessner sent her the melody and she reportedly responded with a fully formed lyrical contribution within around 20 minutes. The song is a dialogue between two lovers rekindling a romance. Thematically similar to her previous Dessner collaboration 'Renegade', Taylor embeds many classic Swiftian themes (of rain, of a dress, of being a problem). Indeed, the opening line of the song sets the scene at a hotel bar (akin to 'Getaway Car's runaway scene). There's wordplay on her request to read her "sentence" – we are left to decide whether she means her written work, or her jail time.

TOP Singer-songwriter Justin Vernon has collaborated with Taylor as part of both Bon Iver and Big Red Machine.

MIDDLE Taylor and the Haim sisters on stage during The Eras Tour.

BOTTOM Performing with Aaron Dessner from The National.